Inter Milan: The Legacy of the Nerazzurri - A Century of Triumph and Tradition

Gigi Romano

Title: Inter Milan: The Legacy of the Nerazzurri—A Century of Triumph and Tradition

Author: Gigi Romano

© **2024. Gigi Romano. All rights reserved.**

No part of this book may be reproduced, distributed, or transmitted in any form or by any means, including photocopying, recording, or other electronic or mechanical methods, without the prior written permission of the publisher, except in the case of brief quotations embodied in critical reviews and certain other noncommercial uses permitted by copyright law. For permission requests, write to the publisher, addressed "Attention: Permissions Coordinator," at the address below.

Disclaimer:

The information in this book is provided for informational purposes only. The author and publisher have made every effort to ensure the accuracy of the information within, but the information contained herein is provided "as is" without warranty, either express or implied. The author and publisher shall not be liable for any losses or damages resulting from the use of the information contained in this book.

First Edition: May, 2020
Second Edition: July, 2022
This Edition: August, 2024

Contents

Introduction
Chapter 1: The Foundation
Chapter 2: Early Achievements
Chapter 3: World War I and Aftermath
Chapter 4: The 1920s
Chapter 5: The Ambrosiana Era
Chapter 6: The 1930s and 1940s
Chapter 7: Post-War Recovery
Chapter 8: The 1950s
Chapter 9: The Arrival of Helenio Herrera
Chapter 10: The Grande Inter Era
Chapter 11: The Decline of Grande Inter
Chapter 12: The 1970s
Chapter 13: The Late 1970s to Early 1980s
Chapter 14: The Trapattoni Era
Chapter 15: The 1990s
Chapter 16: The Moratti Era
Chapter 17: The 2000s
Chapter 18: Post-Mourinho Challenges
Chapter 19: The Zhang Era
Chapter 20: Inter Milan in the 2020s
Chapter 21: The Legacy of Inter Milan
Chapter 22: Inter Milan's Greatest Moments
Chapter 23: The Legends of Inter Milan
Conclusion

Appendices
A. Timeline of Major Events in Inter Milan's History
B. Complete Honors List: Titles and Awards

Bibliography and References

Introduction

Why Inter Milan?

Inter Milan, officially known as Football Club Internazionale Milano, is more than just a football club. It's a symbol of heritage, passion, and an unyielding spirit that has transcended the boundaries of the pitch to become a global phenomenon. From its foundation in 1908 to its status today as one of the most recognized and revered football clubs in the world, Inter Milan has woven a rich tapestry of history, marked by moments of triumph, challenges, and transformation.

Inter Milan's global impact is rooted in its foundation story. The club was born out of a desire for inclusivity and internationalism—a stark contrast to the prevailing nationalism that defined the early 20th century. A group of dissident members from AC Milan, disillusioned by their club's Italian-only player policy, founded Inter Milan with the idea of welcoming players from all over the world. This open-mindedness and international vision are embedded in the club's very name—*Internazionale*—a testament to its founding principles of diversity and openness.

From its inception, Inter Milan has been a beacon of innovation and excellence in football. The club's impact on the sport is immense, influencing tactical evolutions, producing legendary players, and setting standards that other clubs aspire to emulate. Inter's commitment to a distinctive style of play, characterized by technical skill, tactical intelligence, and a relentless pursuit of victory, has made it a reference point in world football.

The influence of Inter Milan extends far beyond the Italian borders. The club's success in European competitions, particularly during the era of *Grande Inter* in the 1960s, established it as a formidable force on the international stage. The back-to-back European Cup victories in 1964 and 1965 under the stewardship of Helenio Herrera solidified Inter Milan's place in the pantheon of footballing greats. These achievements resonated globally, inspiring fans, players, and managers around the world.

Inter Milan's identity as a global club is also reflected in its diverse fanbase. Known as *Nerazzurri* for their iconic black and blue stripes, Inter's supporters are spread across continents, united by their passion for the club. The San Siro, Inter's home for over a century, has become a pilgrimage site for football lovers, a place where the energy of the fans and the history of the club converge to create an electrifying atmosphere. The club's matches, especially the *Derby della Madonnina* against AC Milan, are watched by millions worldwide, symbolizing not just a local rivalry, but a global sporting event.

In recent decades, Inter Milan has continued to evolve, both on and off the field. The club's acquisition by the Suning Holdings Group in 2016 marked a new chapter in its history, reflecting the globalization of football and the growing influence of Asian markets. Under the leadership of Steven Zhang, Inter Milan has not only aimed to reclaim its position at the top of Italian football but also to expand its brand internationally, embracing digital innovations and engaging with a new generation of fans across the globe.

The decision to write about Inter Milan is driven by the desire to capture the essence of a club that is not just a participant in the footballing world but a shaper of it. Inter Milan's history is a rich tapestry of triumphs and tribulations, legends and underdogs, innovation and tradition. It's a story that resonates beyond the confines of sport, touching on broader themes of identity, globalization, and the power of a shared passion.

In exploring the history of Inter Milan, we delve into more than just a series of matches and titles. We uncover the spirit of a club that has consistently strived to balance its local roots with its global aspirations, a club that has faced adversity with resilience, and a club whose legacy continues to inspire and influence the world of football. This book aims to document not only the historical milestones of Inter Milan but also to capture the intangible qualities that make it a unique and enduring symbol in the world of sport.

Chapter 1: The Foundation

The Split from AC Milan (1908)

The origins of Inter Milan are deeply intertwined with the history of its city rival, AC Milan. In the early 20th century, football was rapidly growing in popularity in Italy, particularly in Milan, a city that was becoming a significant industrial and cultural hub. AC Milan, founded in 1899 as the Milan Cricket and Football Club, was one of the leading football clubs in Italy. However, by the first decade of the 20th century, tensions within the club began to simmer, primarily over its restrictive policies regarding player nationality.

AC Milan's management at the time was staunchly Italian in its approach, preferring to field only Italian players. This nationalist sentiment was not uncommon during that period, as many clubs sought to build a strong national identity through sport. However, this exclusionary policy began to create friction within the club, particularly among a group of members who believed that football should transcend national boundaries.

This group of dissenters, consisting of both Italians and Swiss expatriates living in Milan, felt that the club's narrow focus on Italian players was limiting its potential. They envisioned a team that embraced international talent and promoted the idea that football could be a global game. The disagreement over this fundamental issue reached a boiling point in 1908, leading to a split within the club.

On the evening of March 9, 1908, at the *Ristorante Orologio* in Milan, a historic meeting took place. A group of 44 members, led by Giorgio Muggiani, a painter and football enthusiast, decided to break away from AC Milan to form a new club that would embody their ideals. This meeting marked the birth of *Football Club Internazionale Milano*, a name chosen to reflect the new club's commitment to internationalism and openness. The founding members declared that the club would welcome players from all nations, a revolutionary concept at the time.

Giorgio Muggiani, who would also go on to design the club's iconic black and blue striped jersey, expressed the sentiment that drove the formation of Inter Milan: "This wonderful night bestows us with the colors of our crest: black and blue against the golden backdrop of stars. It shall be called Internazionale, because we are brothers of the world." With these words, Inter Milan was born, a club that would not only challenge the established order in Italian football but also promote a broader vision of the sport.

Forming Inter Milan: Ideals and Philosophy (1908-1910)

From its inception, Inter Milan was a club founded on ideals that were progressive and inclusive. The choice of the name *Internazionale* was deliberate, signifying a break from the nationalist tendencies that characterized many other clubs, including AC Milan. Inter's founders were driven by the belief that football should be a game without borders, a sport that brought people together regardless of nationality. This was a bold and innovative idea in an era when national identity often dominated the sports landscape.

Inter Milan's founding philosophy was rooted in the belief that talent should be the only criterion for selecting players, regardless of where they came from. This approach not only allowed the club to attract some of the best talents from across Europe but also set it apart from other Italian clubs, fostering a sense of uniqueness and pride among its supporters. The club quickly gained a reputation for its cosmopolitan outlook, drawing players from Switzerland, Hungary, and other parts of Europe, which was uncommon at the time.

The black and blue stripes of the Inter Milan jersey, designed by Giorgio Muggiani, came to symbolize the club's identity. The black represented night, the blue the sky, and together they symbolized the unity of players and fans under the banner of the club. The crest itself, a circular design with the letters "FCIM" intertwined, became an emblem of the club's commitment to its founding principles.

In the years following its formation, Inter Milan worked hard to establish itself both on and off the pitch. The early years were characterized by a strong commitment to the ideals of internationalism and fair play. The club's management emphasized the importance of sportsmanship, respect for opponents, and the spirit of competition. These values were instilled in the players and became a core part of the club's identity.

On the pitch, Inter Milan quickly made its mark. The club entered the Italian football league system, competing against established teams and proving that its inclusive philosophy could yield success. In 1910, just two

Chapter 1: The Foundation

The Split from AC Milan (1908)

The story of Inter Milan begins with a dramatic and defining moment in the early 20th century—a split that would lead to the birth of one of the most storied football clubs in the world. At the heart of this event was a disagreement over a fundamental issue: the composition of the team. At the time, AC Milan, officially known as the Milan Cricket and Football Club, was one of Italy's leading football institutions. Founded in 1899, the club quickly became a dominant force in Italian football, cultivating a passionate following in Milan.

However, as the club grew, so did internal tensions. By the early 1900s, AC Milan had adopted a policy that prioritized the selection of Italian players, reflecting a broader nationalist sentiment that was prevalent across Europe at the time. This approach, while popular among some, was increasingly seen as restrictive by a faction within the club. This group believed that football, by its very nature, should be an international game, welcoming talent from across the globe.

This ideological divide came to a head in 1908. A group of members, frustrated by the club's insular policy, decided to break away and form a new club.

On the evening of March 9, 1908, at the *Ristorante Orologio* in Milan, 44 members gathered to discuss the future of football in the city. Led by Giorgio Muggiani, a passionate football enthusiast and artist, this group resolved to establish a club that would be open to players of all nationalities. This decision was a bold statement, a rejection of the prevailing norms of the time.

The new club was named *Football Club Internazionale Milano*, a name that reflected its founders' commitment to inclusivity and internationalism. The choice of the name "Internazionale" was not just symbolic; it was a declaration of the club's identity and purpose. Inter Milan was to be a club that stood apart from the rest, embracing players from all over the world and fostering a spirit of unity and brotherhood through football.

Giorgio Muggiani, who would also design the club's first kit, expressed the spirit of the new club: "This wonderful night bestows us with the colors of our crest: black and blue against the golden backdrop of stars. It shall be called Internazionale, because we are brothers of the world." With these words, Inter Milan was born, embodying a vision that would shape the club's future and leave a lasting legacy in world football.

Forming Inter Milan: Ideals and Philosophy (1908-1910)

From its very inception, Inter Milan was built on ideals that were progressive and ahead of their time. The club's founding philosophy was rooted in the belief that football should transcend national boundaries, a radical notion in an era when nationalism often defined sports. The name "Internazionale" was chosen to reflect this belief, signaling a break from the traditionalist and nationalist approaches that characterized many football clubs, including AC Milan.

Inter Milan's founders envisioned a club where the only criteria for selection were talent and ability, regardless of a player's nationality. This inclusive approach allowed the club to attract some of the best talents from across Europe, setting it apart from its contemporaries and establishing a unique identity. The black and blue stripes of the club's kit, designed by Muggiani, symbolized the unity and diversity that the club stood for—black representing night and blue representing the sky, both uniting under the banner of the club's golden crest.

The crest itself, featuring the intertwined initials "FCIM" within a circular design, became an emblem of Inter Milan's commitment to its founding principles. It represented the club's vision of an international community brought together by a shared love of football.

In the early years following its formation, Inter Milan quickly set about establishing itself both on and off the pitch. The club's management and players embraced the values of sportsmanship, respect, and fair competition, which were seen as integral to the club's identity. These principles were not just slogans but were actively cultivated within the team, influencing how players conducted themselves on the field and how the club engaged with its supporters and the broader football community.

On the field, Inter Milan wasted no time in proving that its philosophy could translate into success. The club entered the Italian football league system and quickly became a competitive force, challenging established teams and earning a reputation for its skill and determination. Just two years after its founding, in 1910, Inter Milan won its first Serie A title, a remarkable achievement that underscored the potential of the club's inclusive approach.

This early success was a clear indication that Inter Milan was destined to become a major player in Italian and international football. The club's commitment to its founding ideals of inclusivity, diversity, and internationalism would continue to shape its identity and success for decades to come, laying the foundation for a legacy that would endure well into the 21st century.

Chapter 2: Early Achievements

The First Serie A Title (1910)

Inter Milan's early years were marked by a swift rise to prominence, culminating in the club's first major achievement—the Serie A title in 1910. Just two years after its founding, Inter had already begun to challenge the established powers of Italian football. This rapid ascent was a testament to the vision and determination of its founders, as well as the talent and dedication of its players.

The 1909-1910 season was a pivotal moment in the young club's history. At that time, the Italian football championship was structured quite differently from the modern-day Serie A. The championship was divided into regional groups, with the winners of each group advancing to the national finals. Inter Milan found itself competing in the Northern Italian group, which included some of the strongest teams in the country, such as Pro Vercelli and Genoa, both of whom had already won multiple championships.

Inter's journey to the title was anything but easy. The team faced fierce competition throughout the season, with every match being a critical test of their abilities. As a new club with a bold philosophy, Inter had much to prove. Their success was driven by a combination of tactical innovation, strong team spirit, and the individual brilliance of key players.

One of the standout figures during this period was Virgilio Fossati, Inter Milan's captain and a pivotal player in the club's early history. Fossati was not only a talented midfielder but also a natural leader on the pitch, guiding the team with his vision and tactical acumen. Under his captaincy, Inter Milan developed a style of play that was both effective and attractive, emphasizing teamwork and technical skill.

The climax of the season came when Inter faced Pro Vercelli in the final match to determine the national champion. Pro Vercelli was a formidable opponent, having already established themselves as one of Italy's premier clubs. The match was highly anticipated, with both teams bringing their best to the field. However, Pro Vercelli decided to field a team of young players in protest of a decision by the Italian Football Federation, giving Inter a significant advantage.

Inter Milan capitalized on this opportunity and secured a 10-3 victory, a result that not only secured the championship but also announced the club's arrival on the national stage. Winning the Serie A title in just its second year of existence was a remarkable achievement for Inter Milan. It validated the club's founding ideals and established a foundation for future success. The victory was a moment of immense pride for the club and its supporters, proving that Inter's inclusive and international approach to football could lead to tangible success.

This first title was more than just a trophy; it was a statement of intent. Inter Milan had set out to challenge the status quo, and by winning the Serie A championship, they had done just that. The victory also helped to solidify the club's identity and place within Italian football, earning respect from rivals and recognition from the broader football community.

Challenges in the Early Years (1910-1914)

Despite the early success of winning the Serie A title, the years that followed were challenging for Inter Milan. The club, still in its infancy, faced numerous obstacles as it sought to establish itself as a consistent force in Italian football. The 1910 championship had set high expectations, but maintaining that level of success proved difficult in the face of internal and external challenges.

One of the key challenges during this period was the lack of financial stability. As a relatively new club, Inter Milan did not yet have the financial resources or infrastructure of more established teams. This made it difficult to retain top players and invest in the club's development. The financial constraints were a constant concern for the club's management, who had to be creative in navigating these difficulties while trying to build a competitive team.

On the field, Inter Milan also faced stiff competition from other clubs that were determined to reclaim their dominance. The early 1910s saw the rise of several strong teams, including Pro Vercelli, Casale, and Genoa, each of whom had their own ambitions for national glory. Inter found it challenging to consistently compete at the highest level, and the club's performances in the league were often inconsistent.

In addition to external competition, Inter Milan dealt with internal issues, including changes in management and the inevitable growing pains of a young club. The early years were a time of experimentation and adjustment, as the club worked to refine its playing style and develop a coherent strategy for success. This period also saw fluctuations in the squad, with key players coming and going, further complicating the club's efforts to maintain its early momentum.

Despite these challenges, several key players emerged during this period who would play significant roles in the club's development. Virgilio Fossati continued to be a central figure, not only as a player but also as a leader who embodied the club's ideals. His influence extended beyond the pitch, as he helped to instill a sense of identity and purpose within the team. Tragically, Fossati's career and life were cut short when he was killed in action during World War I, but his legacy would live on as a symbol of the club's early years.

Another important figure was Luigi Amedeo De Vecchi, a versatile defender who became known for his robust playing style and tactical intelligence. De Vecchi was a key part of the team's defense and contributed significantly to Inter's efforts during this challenging period. His leadership at the back was crucial in many of the tough matches that the club faced.

The period from 1910 to 1914 was marked by a mix of highs and lows, as Inter Milan navigated the complexities of establishing itself in a competitive football landscape. While the club did not immediately replicate its early success, these years were crucial in laying the groundwork for future achievements. The challenges faced during this time helped to shape the club's character, fostering a resilience that would become a defining feature of Inter Milan's identity.

As the club moved forward, the lessons learned from these early struggles would prove invaluable. Inter Milan had shown that it could compete with the best, but it also learned that sustained success would require not just talent and vision, but also stability, strategy, and perseverance. These early years set the stage for the growth and evolution of Inter Milan into one of the most successful and iconic football clubs in the world.

Chapter 3: World War I and Aftermath

Inter Milan During World War I (1914-1918)

The outbreak of World War I in 1914 brought about a seismic shift across Europe, affecting every aspect of life, including football. Like many other clubs at the time, Inter Milan found itself deeply affected by the conflict. The war's impact on the club and Italian football was profound, as the sport was forced to take a backseat to the pressing demands of national survival and wartime mobilization.

As the war began, many footballers across Italy were called to serve in the military. Inter Milan was no exception, with several of its key players, including the influential captain Virgilio Fossati, leaving to join the armed forces. The departure of players for military service left clubs like Inter severely weakened, and the football leagues struggled to maintain their schedules. Matches were often postponed or canceled, and the competitive structure of Italian football was significantly disrupted.

Football, once a vibrant and growing sport, became a distant concern as the realities of war took precedence. The Italian Football Federation (FIGC) attempted to continue organizing matches, but the disruptions caused by the war made it increasingly difficult. By 1915, the Italian championship was suspended, and it would not fully resume until after the war's conclusion. During these years, the focus of the nation shifted entirely to the war effort, and the sport was left in a state of dormancy.

For Inter Milan, the war years were marked by loss and uncertainty. The club's operations were severely curtailed, and the absence of regular competition made it difficult to maintain any sense of momentum or continuity. The club's players who had gone to war were no longer available, and many of them, like Fossati, would never return. Virgilio Fossati, who had been a central figure in Inter Milan's early successes, tragically lost his life in 1916 while serving on the front lines. His death was a devastating blow to the club and a poignant reminder of the human cost of the war.

The impact of World War I on Inter Milan was not just felt on the pitch but also in the broader operations of the club. Financial strains became increasingly severe as revenues dwindled without regular matches and competitions. The club's leadership had to navigate these difficult times with limited resources, focusing on keeping the organization intact during the war years. The priorities shifted from growth and competition to mere survival, as the future of the club—and indeed, of the sport itself—became uncertain.

Rebuilding After the War (1918-1920)

When the war finally ended in 1918, Europe was left to pick up the pieces, and football, like many other aspects of life, had to be rebuilt from the ground up. For Inter Milan, the post-war period was one of recovery and renewal, as the club sought to re-establish itself in a vastly changed landscape.

The first step in this rebuilding process was to reassemble a competitive team. With many players having perished or been permanently injured during the war, Inter Milan had to look for new talent. The process of recruiting and training new players was challenging, as the war had created a void in the ranks of experienced footballers across Italy. The club turned to local talents and young prospects, hoping to rebuild the team's strength and cohesion.

The financial situation also needed to be addressed. The war had drained resources, and the club had to find ways to stabilize its finances. This period saw Inter Milan adopting a more cautious approach to its operations, focusing on financial sustainability while gradually rebuilding its competitive edge. The club's leadership worked to secure the necessary funds to support the team and maintain the club's facilities, even as economic conditions in post-war Italy remained difficult.

Despite these challenges, there were key figures who played pivotal roles in guiding Inter Milan through the post-war recovery. One such figure was Leopoldo Conti, a forward who emerged as one of the club's standout players during this time. Conti's skill and leadership on the field were instrumental in helping the club regain its footing in the competitive landscape of Italian football. He became a symbol of the new generation of players who would carry Inter Milan forward into the next decade.

The post-war period also saw the return of organized football competitions in Italy. The Italian Football Federation (FIGC) resumed the national championship, and Inter Milan was eager to participate. However, the club faced stiff competition from other teams that were also rebuilding and looking to establish themselves in the post-war era. The early years of the 1920s were a time of intense competition as clubs across the country sought to reclaim their pre-war status and glory.

Inter Milan's efforts to rebuild were met with both successes and setbacks. The club worked hard to re-establish its presence in the top tier of Italian football, but the path was not easy. The disruption caused by the war had created a highly competitive environment, with many clubs determined to make their mark in the post-war era. Inter Milan had to navigate these challenges while staying true to its founding principles of inclusivity and internationalism.

By 1920, Inter Milan had made significant progress in its recovery efforts. The club had managed to reassemble a competitive team and was once again a force to be reckoned with in Italian football. The resilience shown during this period laid the foundation for future successes, as the club continued to build on the legacy of its early years while adapting to the new realities of post-war Italy.

The rebuilding process after World War I was a crucial period in Inter Milan's history. It was a time of resilience and determination, as the club faced the daunting task of restoring itself in the aftermath of a devastating global conflict. The experiences and lessons learned during these years would prove invaluable as Inter Milan continued to grow and evolve, solidifying its place as one of the most iconic and enduring clubs in the history of football.

Chapter 4: The 1920s

Post-War Resurgence (1920-1925)

As the world emerged from the shadow of World War I, the 1920s marked a period of recovery and renewal, both for society at large and for football clubs like Inter Milan. For Inter, this era was defined by a determined effort to re-establish itself as a competitive force in Italian football after the disruption caused by the war. The club, which had faced significant challenges during the war years, began to rebuild with a sense of purpose and ambition.

The early 1920s were a time of reconstruction for Inter Milan, both on and off the field. The club sought to reclaim its position in the Italian football hierarchy, and this required careful management of resources, strategic player acquisitions, and a renewed focus on developing a cohesive team. With many of its pre-war stars either lost or unable to continue playing, Inter turned to a new generation of players to lead the way.

One of the key figures during this period was Leopoldo Conti, a talented forward who quickly became one of the club's most influential players. Conti's technical skill, creativity, and leadership on the pitch made him a cornerstone of the team's resurgence. His contributions were instrumental in helping Inter Milan regain its competitive edge, as he became a fan favorite and a symbol of the club's post-war revival.

The tactical approach of the team also evolved during these years. Inter Milan adopted a more structured and disciplined style of play, emphasizing teamwork and tactical intelligence. This approach allowed the club to compete effectively against the other top teams in Italy, many of whom were also rebuilding and eager to assert their dominance in the post-war football landscape.

During this period, Inter Milan steadily improved its performance in the Italian championship. The club's resilience and determination were evident as it fought to re-establish itself among the elite teams in the country. While the early 1920s did not bring immediate championship glory, they were crucial in laying the groundwork for future success. Inter Milan's consistent presence in the top tier of Italian football was a testament to the club's ability to overcome adversity and rebuild with a clear sense of direction.

By 1922, Inter Milan had fully re-established itself as a competitive force in Italian football. The club's performances in the league were marked by steady progress, with the team regularly challenging for top positions. The foundation of this resurgence was the combination of emerging talent and experienced leadership, both on and off the pitch. The club's management, recognizing the importance of stability, worked to create an environment where players could develop and thrive.

This period also saw Inter Milan fostering a strong sense of identity and pride among its supporters. The club's black and blue colors, its commitment to internationalism, and its resilience in the face of challenges all contributed to a growing fan base that was deeply loyal to the team. The matches at the San Siro, which had become Inter's home ground in 1926, were characterized by passionate support, as fans rallied behind their team during this crucial phase of its development.

The Rise of Italian Football and Inter's Role (1925-1930)

The latter half of the 1920s witnessed a significant transformation in Italian football, with the sport becoming increasingly popular and competitive across the country. This period was marked by the formalization and professionalization of football in Italy, with clubs, including Inter Milan, playing a crucial role in shaping the future of the sport.

In 1926, a major development occurred with the opening of the San Siro stadium, a new and modern facility that would become synonymous with Inter Milan. The stadium, officially known as Stadio Giuseppe Meazza, was originally built by AC Milan, but Inter soon began sharing the ground, creating a shared footballing icon in the city. The San Siro's capacity and atmosphere made it a fortress for Inter, where fans could gather in large numbers to support their team.

The 1925-1930 period also saw the introduction of the "Giro d'Italia" format, which grouped teams from different regions to compete in a national championship. This new structure aimed to determine the best team in Italy, increasing the stakes and the level of competition. The heightened sense of rivalry and the quest for national supremacy pushed clubs to invest more in their squads, tactics, and infrastructure, leading to a golden era of Italian football.

Inter Milan, now firmly re-established after the challenges of the post-war years, played a central role in this burgeoning football culture. The club's management, recognizing the growing importance of the national championship, sought to strengthen the team further by acquiring top players and refining its tactical approach. The tactical emphasis during this time shifted towards a more organized and methodical style of play, reflecting broader trends in Italian football.

A key figure during this period was Fulvio Bernardini, an intelligent and versatile midfielder who brought both skill and leadership to the team. Bernardini's presence in the midfield helped Inter control the tempo of matches and provided a crucial link between defense and attack. His understanding of the game and ability to dictate play made him one of the standout players of his generation and a key contributor to Inter's success during the late 1920s.

Inter Milan's performances in the national championship during these years were marked by consistency and competitiveness. The club regularly finished near the top of the standings, demonstrating its ability to compete with the best teams in Italy. The 1927-1928 season was particularly notable, as Inter Milan came close to winning the championship, only to be narrowly edged out by Torino. This near-miss fueled the club's determination to achieve greater success in the years to come.

The rise of Italian football during the late 1920s also saw the emergence of intense rivalries, both within Milan and across Italy. The matches between Inter Milan and AC Milan, known as the "Derby della

Madonnina," became some of the most anticipated fixtures of the season, drawing large crowds and creating an electric atmosphere. These derbies were not just battles for local bragging rights but also reflected the broader competition between the two clubs to establish dominance in Italian football.

By the end of the 1920s, Inter Milan had firmly established itself as one of the leading clubs in Italy. The club's role in the development of Italian football during this period was significant, as it contributed to the growth and professionalization of the sport. Inter Milan's commitment to innovation, tactical sophistication, and internationalism continued to define its identity, setting the stage for further successes in the decades to follow.

The 1920s were a crucial decade in Inter Milan's history, marked by a successful resurgence after World War I and a central role in the rise of Italian football. The foundations laid during these years would prove vital as the club continued to evolve, helping to cement Inter Milan's place as one of the most iconic and influential football clubs in the world.

Chapter 5: The Ambrosiana Era

The Fascist Influence and Name Change (1928)

The late 1920s were a time of significant political and social change in Italy, and these shifts inevitably impacted the world of football. The rise of Benito Mussolini's Fascist regime brought about sweeping changes across the country, as the government sought to impose its ideology on all aspects of Italian life, including sports. Football, as the most popular sport in Italy, was seen as a tool for promoting nationalist sentiments and reinforcing the regime's ideals.

In 1928, the Fascist government, in its efforts to align Italian institutions with its nationalist agenda, began to exert pressure on football clubs to adopt names and symbols that reflected Italian heritage and culture. This push for "Italianization" affected many clubs, but none more so than Inter Milan, a club whose very name and identity were rooted in internationalism and inclusivity. The Fascist authorities viewed the name "Internazionale" as a symbol of cosmopolitanism that was at odds with their vision of a unified, nationalist Italy.

Under this pressure, Inter Milan was forced to change its name to *Società Sportiva Ambrosiana*. The new name was chosen to reflect Milan's historical and religious heritage, particularly in reference to Saint Ambrose (*Sant'Ambrogio*), the patron saint of Milan. The name change was more than a mere rebranding; it was a direct challenge to the ideals on which the club had been founded. For many supporters and members of the club, the name "Internazionale" represented a commitment to diversity and openness, and the forced adoption of "Ambrosiana" was seen as a betrayal of these values.

The name change also led to significant changes in the club's identity and image. The iconic black and blue stripes, which had become synonymous with Inter Milan, were replaced by a white shirt featuring a red cross, mirroring the flag of Milan. This alteration further distanced the club from its roots, as it now appeared to align more closely with the Fascist regime's emphasis on nationalism.

The impact of the name change on the club was profound. Many fans and players felt a sense of loss, as the club's original identity was subsumed by the political demands of the time. The change also created a degree of internal conflict, as the club struggled to balance its history and values with the realities of the new political landscape. Despite these challenges, the club continued to compete at the highest level, but the era of Ambrosiana was marked by a sense of unease as the club navigated its way through these turbulent times.

The renaming of Inter Milan to Ambrosiana reflected the broader influence of Fascism on Italian football during this period. The regime sought to control and manipulate the sport to serve its propaganda purposes, using football as a means of promoting national pride and unity. While some clubs adapted to these changes with less resistance, for Inter Milan, the loss of its original name and identity was a painful reminder of the broader impact of Fascism on Italian society.

The Coppa Italia Win (1939)

Despite the challenges posed by the Fascist regime and the forced name change, Ambrosiana-Inter (as the club was eventually known) continued to achieve success on the pitch. The club's resilience and determination during this period were rewarded in 1939, when it secured its first Coppa Italia title, a significant milestone in the club's history.

The Coppa Italia, established in 1922 but not consistently held until the 1930s, was a knockout tournament open to clubs from across Italy. It was a competition that provided an opportunity for teams to prove their prowess outside the regular league structure, offering a chance for glory even if league success proved elusive. For Ambrosiana-Inter, winning the Coppa Italia in 1939 was more than just a triumph on the field; it was a reaffirmation of the club's strength and identity in the face of ongoing political and social pressures.

The road to the 1939 Coppa Italia victory was challenging, as Ambrosiana-Inter faced several formidable opponents throughout the tournament. The team, under the management of Tony Cargnelli, displayed a blend of tactical discipline and individual brilliance that carried them through the competition. The final match was held on June 18, 1939, against Novara, a club that had performed admirably to reach this stage. In a tightly contested match, Ambrosiana-Inter emerged victorious with a 2-1 win, thanks to goals from Pietro Ferraris and Ugo Locatelli.

This victory was significant for several reasons. Firstly, it was the club's first major trophy since the name change, providing a much-needed boost to morale among the players and supporters. The win allowed the club to demonstrate that despite the changes imposed upon it, the spirit of the original Inter Milan still thrived. The triumph also reinforced the club's status as one of Italy's leading football teams, capable of competing at the highest level and achieving success even in difficult circumstances.

The Coppa Italia win was also important in the context of Italian football. By the late 1930s, the Fascist regime had deeply embedded itself into all aspects of society, including sports. For Ambrosiana-Inter, winning the Coppa Italia was not only a sporting achievement but also a subtle act of defiance—a way of preserving the club's legacy and demonstrating its resilience in the face of external pressures.

The significance of the 1939 Coppa Italia victory extended beyond the immediate joy of winning a trophy. It served as a reminder of the club's enduring strength and its ability to overcome adversity. For the fans, it was a moment of pride, reinforcing their connection to the club and its history. The victory also provided a foundation upon which future successes would be built, as the club continued to navigate the complex political landscape of Italy in the years leading up to World War II.

In retrospect, the Ambrosiana era, while marked by political interference and challenges to the club's identity, also highlighted the resilience and determination of Inter Milan. The forced name change and the Coppa Italia victory in 1939 were symbolic of the broader struggles and triumphs that the club experienced during this period. As the world moved closer to another global conflict, Ambrosiana-Inter stood as a testament to the enduring power of football and the unbreakable spirit of a club that refused to be defined by external forces.

The Ambrosiana era came to an end after World War II, when the club was finally able to reclaim its original name and identity. However, the experiences of this period left a lasting impact on Inter Milan, shaping its character and reinforcing the values that had guided its founding. The Coppa Italia win of 1939 remains a cherished memory in the club's history, a reminder of the resilience and pride that has always defined Inter Milan, even in its darkest moments.

Chapter 6: The 1930s and 1940s

Inter Milan's Struggles in the 1930s (1930-1939)

The 1930s were a tumultuous period for Inter Milan, a decade marked by both internal challenges and external pressures. After the club's forced name change to Ambrosiana in 1928 under the Fascist regime, the 1930s continued to present a complex set of difficulties that tested the club's resilience and adaptability.

The early part of the decade saw Inter Milan, then known as Ambrosiana, struggling to maintain its competitive edge in a rapidly evolving football landscape. The name change imposed by the Fascist government was more than just a cosmetic alteration; it was a symbolic shift that many within the club found difficult to reconcile with their original ideals. The forced adoption of a more nationalistic identity created a sense of alienation among some players and fans, which in turn affected morale and performance.

On the pitch, the club faced fierce competition from other Italian teams that were also improving their squads and tactics. Clubs like Juventus, Bologna, and Torino emerged as formidable opponents, making it increasingly difficult for Ambrosiana to consistently compete for the top positions in the league. The tactical innovations that had characterized Italian football during this period, such as the adoption of the "metodo" system (a precursor to the modern 3-2-2-3 formation), required teams to adapt quickly, but Ambrosiana often found itself lagging behind its rivals in implementing these changes effectively.

Another significant challenge during the 1930s was the frequent turnover of players and coaches. The club struggled to find a stable and consistent leadership both on and off the field, which hindered its ability to develop a coherent strategy for success. The constant changes in personnel disrupted the team's chemistry and made it difficult to build a sustained challenge for the championship.

Despite these struggles, there were still moments of promise. The club managed to win the Serie A title in the 1937-1938 season, a significant achievement considering the difficulties of the preceding years. This success was largely attributed to the tactical acumen of coach Armando Castellazzi and the performances of key players like Giuseppe Meazza, one of the greatest Italian footballers of all time. Meazza, who was the club's star forward, played a pivotal role in leading the team to victory, his brilliance on the pitch often masking the underlying issues within the squad.

However, the joy of this title was somewhat fleeting, as the challenges continued into the following season. Ambrosiana struggled to replicate its success, and the inconsistency that had plagued the club earlier in the decade resurfaced. The inability to build on their 1938 title win was indicative of the deeper issues that the club faced—issues that were exacerbated by the political climate and the impending global conflict.

The 1930s were also a time of financial difficulties for many Italian football clubs, including Ambrosiana. The economic policies of the Fascist regime, combined with the broader global economic depression, put a strain on the club's finances. This financial instability affected the club's ability to invest in new players and infrastructure, further hampering its efforts to remain competitive at the highest level.

By the end of the decade, Ambrosiana had weathered a series of challenges that left it in a precarious position. The club's struggles in the 1930s highlighted the difficulties of maintaining success in a rapidly changing environment, both on the football field and in the broader political landscape. These challenges set the stage for an even more difficult period as the world plunged into the turmoil of World War II.

Inter Milan During World War II (1939-1945)

The outbreak of World War II in 1939 brought about a dramatic shift in the lives of people across the globe, and football, like many other aspects of life, was deeply affected. For Inter Milan, still officially known as Ambrosiana, the war years were a time of great difficulty and uncertainty, as the club faced numerous challenges both on and off the field.

As the war intensified, many football players were called up for military service, leaving clubs severely depleted. Ambrosiana, like other teams, lost a significant portion of its squad to the war effort. The absence of key players made it difficult to field a competitive team, and the quality of football inevitably suffered. Matches continued to be played, but they were often disrupted by the realities of wartime, including air raids, travel restrictions, and shortages of basic resources.

The Italian football championship was severely disrupted during the war years. The 1942-1943 season was the last full season before the championship was suspended due to the war. The subsequent seasons saw the league structure collapse, with only regional competitions taking place sporadically. The situation was chaotic, and many clubs struggled to maintain any semblance of normalcy. For Ambrosiana, this meant focusing on survival rather than success, as the club, like many others, had to adapt to the ever-changing circumstances.

Off the pitch, the club faced significant financial difficulties. The war strained the Italian economy, and football clubs, which were already operating on tight budgets, found it increasingly hard to stay afloat. Ambrosiana had to make tough decisions to keep the club running, including cutting costs wherever possible. The lack of regular competition also meant a decline in revenue, as ticket sales and other sources of income dwindled.

Despite these challenges, Ambrosiana remained committed to preserving the club's spirit and identity. The management and remaining players worked tirelessly to keep the club alive, even as the war raged on. The San Siro stadium, which had become a symbol of the club, was used for various purposes during the war, including as a makeshift shelter during air raids. The stadium, like the club itself, stood as a testament to the resilience of those who refused to let the war destroy what they had built.

One of the most difficult aspects of the war years was the uncertainty about the future. With Italy caught in the turmoil of the conflict and the Fascist regime increasingly isolated, it was unclear what would happen to Italian football once the war ended. For Ambrosiana, the challenge was not only to survive the war but also to prepare for an unknown future.

As the war drew to a close in 1945, Italy was left devastated, and the country faced the enormous task of rebuilding. For Ambrosiana, the end of the war marked the beginning of a new chapter, one that would see the club reclaim its original name and identity. The post-war period would bring its own set of challenges, but the experiences of the 1930s and 1940s had forged a resilience in the club that would serve it well in the years to come.

The 1930s and 1940s were a period of profound struggle for Inter Milan, marked by political interference, financial difficulties, and the impact of a world at war. Despite these challenges, the club's determination to survive and its ability to adapt to changing circumstances allowed it to emerge from this difficult period with its spirit intact. The lessons learned during these years would prove invaluable as the club entered the post-war era, ready to rebuild and reassert itself as one of Italy's premier football institutions.

Chapter 7: Post-War Recovery

Rebuilding the Club After World War II (1945-1948)

The end of World War II in 1945 marked the beginning of a new era for Europe, as nations embarked on the difficult task of rebuilding their societies from the devastation of conflict. For Inter Milan, the post-war period was a time of significant change and recovery. The club, like many others across Italy, had been severely impacted by the war, both on and off the pitch. The immediate challenge was to rebuild a team and organization that had been fragmented by years of war and hardship.

One of the first steps in the post-war recovery was to reclaim the club's original identity. The name "Ambrosiana," which had been imposed by the Fascist regime in 1928, was officially dropped, and the club proudly returned to its original name: *Football Club Internazionale Milano*. This change was more than symbolic; it represented a return to the club's founding principles of internationalism and inclusivity. For the players, staff, and supporters, the restoration of the name "Inter" was a powerful affirmation of the club's enduring spirit and values, even after years of political and social upheaval.

However, the challenges of rebuilding went far beyond the restoration of a name. The club faced significant financial difficulties in the immediate post-war period. Italy, like much of Europe, was economically devastated, and football clubs struggled to find the resources needed to operate effectively. For Inter, this meant carefully managing limited funds while attempting to rebuild a competitive squad. The club's management focused on stabilizing finances and securing the resources needed to move forward.

Reconstructing the team itself was a daunting task. Many players had been lost to the war, either through death, injury, or retirement. The talent pool was severely depleted, and the club had to search for new players who could restore Inter Milan to its former glory. This search was not limited to Italy; true to its international roots, Inter began to look beyond the country's borders to find players who could contribute to the club's resurgence.

One of the key figures in this rebuilding process was Carlo Masseroni, who took over as president of the club in 1947. Masseroni was instrumental in guiding Inter through the challenging post-war years, focusing on both the financial stability of the club and the development of a competitive team. Under his leadership, Inter began to regain its footing in

Italian football, laying the foundation for future successes.

On the pitch, the immediate post-war years were characterized by a mix of rebuilding and experimentation. The team, which was still in the process of re-establishing itself, had to navigate the complexities of a league that was also recovering from the war. The 1945-1946 season was the first full season after the war, and it was marked by an expanded league structure to accommodate the many clubs returning to competition. Inter Milan's performances during this period were inconsistent, as the club worked to regain its pre-war form and establish a cohesive team.

Despite the challenges, there were positive signs of progress. Inter managed to secure respectable finishes in the league, demonstrating that the club was on the right track. The recruitment of new players and the return of football to the San Siro stadium, which had survived the war largely intact, helped to restore a sense of normalcy and optimism. The stadium once again became a gathering place for supporters, who were eager to see their team rise to prominence once more.

Return to Competitiveness (1948-1950)

As the 1940s drew to a close, Inter Milan began to show clear signs of a resurgence. The club, having successfully navigated the immediate challenges of the post-war period, was now focused on returning to the upper echelons of Italian football. This period marked the beginning of a new chapter for Inter, one characterized by renewed ambition and a determination to reclaim the success that had eluded the club during the difficult war years.

One of the pivotal moments in this resurgence was the appointment of Giulio Cappelli as coach in 1948. Cappelli, a former player with a deep understanding of the game, brought a fresh perspective to the team. He emphasized discipline, tactical awareness, and a strong work ethic, qualities that were essential for a team that was still rebuilding. Under his guidance, Inter Milan began to develop a more cohesive and effective style of play, one that could compete with the best teams in the league.

The 1948-1949 season was a turning point for Inter Milan. The club had managed to strengthen its squad with key signings, including the acquisition of Benito Lorenzi, a talented forward who would become one of the club's most iconic players. Lorenzi's arrival brought a new dynamism to Inter's attack, and his partnership with the likes of Amedeo Amadei and István Nyers provided the team with a potent offensive threat. Lorenzi's fierce determination and technical skill quickly made him a fan favorite, and he played a crucial role in driving the team forward.

The improvement in the squad's quality was reflected in the club's performances on the pitch. Inter Milan finished the 1948-1949 season in a strong third place, a significant achievement considering the challenges of the previous years. The team's success was built on a solid defense, led by the experienced Carlo Annovazzi, and a creative midfield that could control the tempo of matches. This combination of defensive solidity and attacking flair allowed Inter to compete effectively against the top teams in Italy.

The 1949-1950 season saw further progress, as Inter Milan continued to build on the foundations laid in the previous year. The club's performances were marked by consistency and determination, qualities that had been instilled by Cappelli and the new wave of players who had joined the team. Inter finished the season as runners-up in Serie A, just behind Juventus, signaling that the club was once again a serious contender for the championship.

This return to competitiveness was a testament to the hard work and resilience of everyone involved with Inter Milan. The players, coaches, and management had all contributed to the club's revival, overcoming the difficulties of the post-war years to restore the team to its rightful place in Italian football. The support of the fans, who had remained loyal throughout the challenging times, was also crucial, as their unwavering belief in the club provided a source of inspiration for the team.

The period from 1948 to 1950 was crucial in setting the stage for the successes that would follow in the coming years. Inter Milan had not only re-established itself as a top club in Italy but had also laid the groundwork for a new era of triumphs. The club's ability to rebuild after the war and return to competitiveness was a reflection of its enduring spirit and its commitment to the values that had defined it since its founding.

As the 1950s approached, Inter Milan was poised to enter a period of sustained success, with a strong team, a clear vision, and a renewed sense of purpose. The experiences of the post-war years had forged a resilience and determination that would serve the club well as it pursued its ambitions in the years to come. The return to competitiveness was not just about winning matches; it was about reclaiming the identity and pride of a club that had always strived to be at the forefront of Italian and international football.

Chapter 8: The 1950s

The Early 1950s: Rising to Dominance (1950-1954)

The 1950s marked the beginning of a golden era for Inter Milan, a period characterized by rising dominance in Italian football and the consolidation of the club's status as one of Europe's elite teams. The early years of this decade were pivotal, as Inter Milan began to build on the momentum gained in the late 1940s, laying the foundation for sustained success.

The 1950-1951 season was a clear indication that Inter Milan was ready to challenge for the top honors in Italian football. Under the management of Alfredo Foni, who took charge in 1952, Inter adopted a tactical approach that emphasized a strong, disciplined defense, combined with a direct and effective attacking strategy. Foni, a former Italian international, brought with him a wealth of experience and a clear vision for the team, which proved instrumental in guiding Inter to new heights.

A key figure during this period was the Hungarian forward István Nyers, who had joined the club in 1948. Nyers quickly established himself as one of the most lethal strikers in Serie A, known for his pace, powerful shots, and clinical finishing. His ability to consistently find the back of the net made him a crucial asset for Inter Milan, and he played a significant role in the club's rise to prominence in the early 1950s. Nyers' partnership with Amedeo Amadei, another prolific forward, gave Inter one of the most feared attacking duos in the league.

The early 1950s also saw the emergence of several other key players who would define this era. Among them was the talented winger Lennart Skoglund, a Swedish international who brought flair and creativity to Inter's play. Skoglund's dribbling skills and ability to deliver precise crosses made him a fan favorite and an integral part of the team's success. His presence on the left wing provided balance to the attack, complementing the goal-scoring prowess of Nyers and Amadei.

Inter Milan's performances during this period were characterized by consistency and resilience. The team's ability to grind out results, even in difficult matches, was a testament to the tactical discipline instilled by Foni. One of the most memorable matches of this era came in the 1952-1953 season when Inter Milan defeated Juventus 3-1 in a crucial encounter that solidified their position at the top of the table. This victory not only highlighted the team's quality but also reinforced their credentials as genuine title contenders.

The 1952-1953 season culminated in Inter Milan winning the Serie A title, their first Scudetto since 1938. The achievement was a significant milestone for the club, marking the beginning of a period of dominance in Italian football. The team's success was built on a solid defense, an effective midfield, and a potent attack, all of which worked in harmony to deliver the club's first post-war championship. The Scudetto win was a clear indication that Inter Milan was back at the top, ready to challenge for more honors in the years to come.

The following season, 1953-1954, saw Inter Milan successfully defend their title, securing back-to-back Scudetti for the first time in the club's history. This period of dominance was a testament to the team's quality and the effectiveness of Foni's tactical approach. The consistency shown by Inter during these years was remarkable, as they established themselves as the team to beat in Italian football. The consecutive title wins also reinforced the club's growing reputation on the European stage, as Inter began to be recognized as one of the continent's leading clubs.

The Impact of Foreign Players (1954-1958)

The mid-1950s were a time of significant change and evolution for Inter Milan, marked by the increasing influence of foreign players on the team's fortunes.

While the club had always maintained an international outlook, true to its name *Internazionale*, this period saw a deliberate strategy to bring in top talent from abroad to strengthen the squad and maintain its competitive edge.

One of the most influential foreign players to join Inter during this period was the Brazilian midfielder Jair da Costa. Jair arrived at Inter in 1957, bringing with him a unique blend of flair, technical ability, and creativity that added a new dimension to the team's play. His ability to dribble past opponents, deliver accurate crosses, and score crucial goals made him an invaluable addition to the squad. Jair's impact was immediate, as he quickly became a key player for Inter, contributing to the team's attacking prowess.

Another significant foreign acquisition was Austrian forward Ernst Ocwirk, who joined Inter Milan in 1956. Ocwirk was known for his tactical intelligence, versatility, and leadership on the field. His ability to play both as a midfielder and as a forward made him a crucial asset for Inter, and his experience added a level of maturity to the squad. Ocwirk's presence in the team helped Inter maintain its competitive edge in the increasingly tough environment of Serie A.

These foreign players brought not only their individual skills but also new ideas and styles of play that enriched Inter Milan's tactical approach. The blend of Italian and foreign talent created a diverse and dynamic squad capable of competing at the highest level. The arrival of these players also reflected the club's ambition to remain at the forefront of Italian and European football, as they sought to build a team that could challenge for titles both domestically and internationally.

However, the integration of foreign players also presented challenges. The team had to adapt to different playing styles and personalities, which required careful management to ensure cohesion on the pitch. Coach Foni and his successors worked to blend the various talents into a unified team, balancing the need for individual brilliance with the importance of teamwork and discipline.

The impact of these foreign players was evident in Inter Milan's performances during the latter half of the 1950s. While the club did not immediately replicate its earlier success in terms of winning titles, the quality of football improved, and the team remained a formidable force in Serie A. The presence of international stars helped to raise the club's profile, attracting more attention from fans and media alike.

The 1957 Scudetto: A Turning Point

The 1956-1957 season was a pivotal one in the history of Inter Milan, culminating in a league title that marked a turning point for the club. After a few years of near misses and intense competition, Inter Milan once again claimed the Serie A championship, securing their third Scudetto of the decade and their ninth overall.

The 1957 Scudetto was significant for several reasons. First and foremost, it reaffirmed Inter Milan's position as one of the dominant forces in Italian football. The title win was the result of consistent performances throughout the season, with the team demonstrating both attacking flair and defensive solidity. The contributions of key players like Nyers, Lorenzi, and the recently acquired foreign stars were crucial in securing the championship.

One of the defining features of the 1957 title-winning team was its balance. The defense, led by captain Ivano Blason, was one of the best in the league, while the midfield and attack worked seamlessly to create and convert scoring opportunities. This balance allowed Inter Milan to navigate the challenges of a long and competitive season, ultimately emerging as the best team in Italy.

The 1957 Scudetto also marked a turning point in the club's history because it set the stage for the next phase of Inter Milan's development. The success of the 1950s laid the groundwork for the era of *Grande Inter* in the 1960s, a period of unprecedented dominance under the legendary coach Helenio Herrera. The 1957 title win demonstrated that Inter Milan had the quality and ambition to compete at the highest level, and it provided the confidence and momentum needed to build a team capable of achieving even greater success.

Moreover, the 1957 Scudetto was significant in that it signaled a shift in the club's approach to building a team. The success achieved with a blend of Italian and foreign talent highlighted the importance of scouting and recruiting top players from around the world. This strategy would become a cornerstone of Inter Milan's future successes, as the club continued to attract some of the best players from Europe and beyond.

The title win was celebrated with great enthusiasm by the club's supporters, who had witnessed their team overcome the challenges of the previous years to reclaim its place at the top of Italian football. The victory parade through the streets of Milan was a jubilant affair, as fans came out in large numbers to celebrate the achievement of their beloved team.

The 1957 Scudetto was a moment of pride for everyone associated with Inter Milan, from the players and coaches to the management and fans.

In retrospect, the 1957 league title was more than just a trophy; it was a symbol of Inter Milan's resilience, ambition, and ability to adapt to changing circumstances. It marked the culmination of years of hard work and set the stage for the club's future successes. As the 1950s came to a close, Inter Milan stood on the brink of a new era, ready to build on the foundations laid during this remarkable decade and to continue its pursuit of greatness in the years to come.

Chapter 9: The Arrival of Helenio Herrera

Hiring Helenio Herrera (1960)

The arrival of Helenio Herrera at Inter Milan in 1960 marked a transformative moment in the club's history, setting the stage for one of the most successful and influential periods in European football. Herrera's appointment as head coach was the result of a deliberate and strategic decision by Inter's management, led by club president Angelo Moratti, to elevate the team to new heights and to establish Inter Milan as a dominant force in both Italian and international football.

The late 1950s had been a period of relative success for Inter Milan, with the club securing several league titles and maintaining a strong presence in Serie A. However, the club's ambitions extended beyond domestic success. Angelo Moratti, who had taken over as president in 1955, was determined to build a team that could compete with the best in Europe and to bring the prestigious European Cup to Milan. To achieve this goal, Moratti knew that he needed a coach with not only tactical acumen but also the charisma and leadership qualities necessary to mold a group of talented players into a cohesive, winning team.

Helenio Herrera, a coach with a growing reputation in European football, was identified as the ideal candidate for this role. Born in Buenos Aires to Spanish parents, Herrera had already enjoyed success in Spain, winning La Liga titles with both Atlético Madrid and Barcelona. His coaching style was characterized by meticulous attention to detail, a deep understanding of tactics, and an ability to motivate players to perform at their highest level. Herrera was also known for his strong personality and his belief in discipline, both on and off the pitch.

Moratti's decision to bring Herrera to Inter Milan was not just about tactics; it was about instilling a new culture at the club. Herrera's reputation as a disciplinarian and his emphasis on physical fitness, psychological preparation, and teamwork aligned perfectly with Moratti's vision for the club. The appointment of Herrera in 1960 was seen as a bold move, but one that underscored Inter's determination to compete at the highest level and to build a team capable of winning the European Cup.

Herrera's arrival was met with a mix of excitement and skepticism. While his success in Spain was undeniable, the question remained whether he could replicate that success in the more defensively oriented Serie A. However, Herrera quickly set about proving his doubters wrong. His first task was to assess the squad and identify areas for improvement. Herrera was known for his rigorous training methods and his demand for absolute commitment from his players. He believed in creating a strong, unified team where every player understood their role and was prepared to work for the collective success of the team.

Herrera's influence was immediate, as he began to implement changes both on and off the pitch. He introduced new training regimes, emphasizing fitness, tactical awareness, and psychological preparation. Herrera's attention to detail was legendary; he was known to meticulously study opponents, preparing his team with detailed instructions on how to counter their strengths and exploit their weaknesses. This approach quickly won him the respect of the players, who began to buy into his philosophy and vision for the team.

The Early Impact of Herrera's Strategies (1960-1962)

One of the most significant aspects of Herrera's early tenure at Inter Milan was his introduction of the *Catenaccio* system, a tactical approach that would come to define the club's style of play during the 1960s. While *Catenaccio* had its roots in earlier tactical systems, Herrera refined and perfected it, making it a cornerstone of Inter Milan's success. The term *Catenaccio*, which means "chain" in Italian, referred to the system's emphasis on defensive solidity and organization, with a focus on counter-attacking football.

At the heart of Herrera's *Catenaccio* was the *libero* or sweeper, a free-roaming defender who played behind the main defensive line. This player was responsible for sweeping up any loose balls and providing an additional layer of security at the back. Herrera's innovation was to combine this defensive structure with a highly disciplined and organized midfield and attack, ensuring that the team could quickly transition from defense to attack, often catching opponents off guard with rapid counter-attacks.

The key to the success of *Catenaccio* was its flexibility. While the system was primarily defensive, it allowed for quick and effective counter-attacking moves, often involving only a few players who could exploit the spaces left by the opposition. Herrera drilled his players relentlessly in this system, ensuring that they understood their roles and responsibilities within the framework. The emphasis on defensive organization did not mean sacrificing attacking prowess; rather, it was about being efficient and clinical when opportunities arose.

The early impact of Herrera's strategies was evident in Inter Milan's performances during the 1960-1962 period. The team quickly became known for its defensive strength, with opponents finding it increasingly difficult to break down Inter's well-organized backline. The introduction of *Catenaccio* also brought about a more cohesive and disciplined style of play, with every player fully aware of their role within the team. Herrera's insistence on physical fitness and mental preparation meant that Inter's players were not only tactically astute but also among the fittest in the league.

One of the most significant matches that demonstrated the effectiveness of Herrera's approach was Inter Milan's victory over Juventus in the 1960-1961 season. Juventus, one of Inter's fiercest rivals, had been dominating Italian football, but Herrera's Inter team executed the *Catenaccio* system to perfection, securing a crucial 3-1 win that signaled the arrival of a new force in Serie A. This victory was a turning point, as it showed that Inter Milan was capable of challenging the established order and that Herrera's methods were yielding results.

The 1961-1962 season saw further improvements, with Inter Milan finishing second in Serie A, just behind AC Milan. While the team narrowly missed out on the title, the season was marked by significant progress, both in terms of results and the development of a winning mentality. The players had fully embraced Herrera's philosophy, and the team was now a well-oiled machine, capable of executing the *Catenaccio* system with precision.

By the end of the 1961-1962 season, it was clear that Herrera's arrival had fundamentally transformed Inter Milan. The club was now a disciplined, tactically sophisticated team, capable of competing at the highest level in Italy and Europe. The groundwork had been laid for what would become one of the most successful periods in the club's history—the era of *Grande Inter*, where Herrera's vision and leadership would guide the team to unprecedented success.

The early impact of Herrera's strategies not only redefined Inter Milan's style of play but also set a new standard in European football. The introduction of *Catenaccio* and the emphasis on discipline, fitness, and tactical awareness became hallmarks of Inter Milan's identity during the 1960s. As the team prepared for the challenges ahead, there was a growing sense of belief that under Herrera's guidance, Inter Milan could achieve greatness. The stage was set for the club's ascent to the pinnacle of European football, a journey that would begin with

Herrera's tactical revolution and his unyielding pursuit of excellence.

Chapter 10: The Grande Inter Era

Building the Grande Inter (1962-1964)

The early 1960s marked the beginning of a golden era for Inter Milan, a period that would come to be known as the *Grande Inter* era. Under the leadership of Helenio Herrera, the club embarked on a journey that would transform it into one of the most dominant and respected teams in the history of European football. The period between 1962 and 1964 was crucial in building the foundation of this legendary team, which would go on to achieve unprecedented success both domestically and internationally.

After two seasons of laying the groundwork and implementing his tactical philosophies, Herrera began to shape the squad according to his vision. Recognizing the need for a balanced team that could execute his *Catenaccio* system with precision, Herrera, alongside club president Angelo Moratti, focused on assembling a group of players who possessed the necessary technical skills, tactical intelligence, and mental toughness.

One of the cornerstones of this team was Giacinto Facchetti, a young defender who would become one of the greatest full-backs in the history of the game. Facchetti was a perfect fit for Herrera's system, combining defensive solidity with an exceptional ability to contribute to the attack. His pace, athleticism, and vision allowed him to play a key role in both shutting down opposition wingers and initiating counter-attacks, making him an integral part of the team's success.

In midfield, Herrera relied on the leadership and creativity of Luis Suárez, a Spanish playmaker who had been a key figure in Herrera's success at Barcelona. Suárez was the heartbeat of the team, dictating the tempo of the game with his precise passing and tactical awareness. His ability to control the midfield and link up with both the defense and attack was crucial to the effectiveness of *Catenaccio*, making him one of the most important players in the team.

The defensive backbone of the team was anchored by Armando Picchi, who played as the *libero* or sweeper in Herrera's system. Picchi's role was pivotal in organizing the defense and providing an extra layer of security behind the backline. His reading of the game, positional sense, and leadership on the field made him the perfect fit for the *libero* role, allowing the rest of the defense to function with confidence and precision.

Up front, Sandro Mazzola emerged as one of the team's most potent attacking threats. Mazzola, the son of the legendary Valentino Mazzola, possessed a blend of skill, speed, and intelligence that made him a constant danger to opposing defenses. His ability to score goals, create opportunities for his teammates, and deliver in crucial moments made him one of the standout players of the *Grande Inter* era.

With these key players, along with a supporting cast that included Tarcisio Burgnich, Mario Corso, and Jair da Costa, Herrera had assembled a team that was not only tactically astute but also mentally resilient and capable of handling the pressure of top-level competition. The 1962-1963 season saw Inter Milan narrowly miss out on the Serie A title, finishing second, but the team's performances indicated that something special was brewing.

The 1963-1964 season would prove to be a defining one for Inter Milan. The team, now fully attuned to Herrera's system, played with a level of discipline and efficiency that few teams could match. Inter Milan won the Serie A title, securing their place as the top team in Italy. But it was in Europe where the team would truly make its mark, setting the stage for one of the greatest achievements in the club's history.

The 1964 European Cup Win

The 1963-1964 European Cup campaign was a momentous one for Inter Milan, as the club embarked on a journey to claim its first European title. The European Cup, the precursor to the modern UEFA Champions League, was the most prestigious competition in European club football, bringing together the champions of the continent's top leagues. Winning this tournament was the ultimate goal for any club aspiring to be recognized as the best in Europe.

Inter Milan's path to the final was anything but easy. The competition featured some of the strongest teams in Europe, including Real Madrid, who had dominated the tournament in its early years. However, Herrera's team approached each match with a meticulous game plan, combining defensive solidity with swift and deadly counter-attacks. The players executed the *Catenaccio* system to perfection, frustrating opponents with their organization and discipline.

The semi-final against Borussia Dortmund was a stern test for Inter Milan. The German side was known for their attacking prowess, but Inter's defense, led by Picchi and supported by Facchetti and Burgnich, held firm. In the first leg, Inter secured a 2-2 draw away from home, setting up a decisive return leg at the San Siro. In front of a passionate home crowd, Inter Milan delivered a masterclass in defensive football, winning 2-0 and securing their place in the final.

The final, held on May 27, 1964, at the Praterstadion in Vienna, pitted Inter Milan against the Spanish giants Real Madrid. Real Madrid, winners of five European Cups in the previous eight years, were the favorites, boasting a squad filled with stars like Alfredo Di Stéfano and Ferenc Puskás. However, Herrera's Inter Milan entered the match with confidence, fully aware of their own strengths and well-prepared to counter Madrid's attacking threats.

Inter Milan's performance in the final was a showcase of everything that made the *Grande Inter* team special. The match started with a goal from Sandro Mazzola, who scored in the 10th minute, giving Inter an early lead. Real Madrid, despite their attacking firepower, found it difficult to break down Inter's disciplined defense. Picchi and his fellow defenders kept Di Stéfano and Puskás at bay, while Suárez controlled the midfield, dictating the tempo of the game.

Inter Milan doubled their lead in the second half with a goal from Aurelio Milani, further solidifying their control of the match. Real Madrid managed to pull one back, but Mazzola quickly restored the two-goal cushion with his second goal of the match, sealing a 3-1 victory for Inter Milan. The final whistle sparked scenes of jubilation among the Inter players, coaching staff, and fans, as the club celebrated its first European Cup triumph.

The 1964 European Cup win was a historic achievement for Inter Milan. It was not only the club's first European title but also a validation of Herrera's tactical genius and the effectiveness of the *Catenaccio* system. The victory established Inter Milan as a force to be reckoned with in European football and solidified the club's place among the elite. The triumph also marked the culmination of years of hard work, dedication, and a relentless pursuit of excellence by Herrera and his players.

For the fans, the 1964 European Cup win was a moment of immense pride. It was a confirmation that their club had reached the pinnacle of European football, and it created a bond between the team and its supporters that would endure for generations. The victory in Vienna was the first of what would become a series of European successes, as Inter Milan set its sights on maintaining its dominance in the years to come.

Back-to-Back European Successes (1965-1966)

Following their historic European Cup win in 1964, Inter Milan entered the 1964-1965 season with a new sense of purpose and determination. The challenge now was to defend their European title while continuing to dominate domestically. The team, now fully matured under Herrera's guidance, was ready to take on the best that Europe had to offer.

The 1964-1965 European Cup campaign was marked by a series of impressive performances from Inter Milan. The team navigated through the tournament with the same discipline and tactical mastery that had brought them success the previous year. One of the most notable victories came in the semi-finals, where Inter faced Liverpool. After a 3-1 defeat at Anfield in the first leg, Inter Milan produced one of the most memorable comebacks in European Cup history, winning the return leg 3-0 at the San Siro to secure their place in the final.

The final, held on May 27, 1965, at the San Siro, was a home fixture for Inter Milan, giving them a significant advantage. The opponents were Benfica, the reigning champions of Portugal and one of the top teams in Europe. Despite the high stakes, Inter Milan remained calm and focused, executing Herrera's game plan with precision. A solitary goal from Jair da Costa in the 42nd minute was enough to secure a 1-0 victory, allowing Inter Milan to retain the European Cup.

Winning back-to-back European Cups was a monumental achievement, something only a few clubs had managed to do at the time. The 1965 victory reinforced Inter Milan's status as the best team in Europe and solidified the legacy of the *Grande Inter* era. Herrera's team had now firmly established themselves as a dynasty, with their blend of defensive organization and clinical counter-attacking proving too much for their European rivals.

The 1965-1966 season saw Inter Milan continuing their dominance in European football. Once again, the team reached the final of the European Cup, this time facing the Spanish champions, Real Madrid. The final, held on May 11, 1966, at the Heysel Stadium in Brussels, was a chance for Inter Milan to make history by winning their third consecutive European Cup.

In a hard-fought match, Inter Milan's defense, as always, was rock-solid, with Picchi and Facchetti leading the backline. However, this time, Real Madrid managed to break through, and despite Inter's best efforts, the Spanish side emerged victorious with a 2-1 win. Although Inter Milan fell short of a third consecutive European title, their achievement in reaching three consecutive finals and winning two of them remains one of the most remarkable accomplishments in the history of the competition.

The impact of these back-to-back European successes on Inter Milan was profound. The club had not only established itself as a powerhouse in Italy but also as one of the most feared and respected teams in Europe. The *Grande Inter* era had created a legacy that would endure for decades, influencing the way football was played and leaving an indelible mark on the sport's history.

The back-to-back European Cup victories also cemented Helenio Herrera's reputation as one of the greatest football managers of all time. His tactical innovations, particularly the use of *Catenaccio*, and his ability to get the best out of his players, had brought unprecedented success to Inter Milan. The *Grande Inter* era under Herrera is remembered not just for the titles won, but for the way the team played—combining discipline, strategy, and flair in a way that few teams had done before.

For the players who were part of this era, the experience was unforgettable. They had been part of a team that achieved greatness, and their names became synonymous with the club's most successful period. The triumphs of the 1960s created a bond between the players, the club, and the fans that would last a lifetime, as they collectively celebrated the achievements of one of the greatest teams in football history.

The *Grande Inter* era, with its European successes, remains a defining chapter in the history of Inter Milan. It was a time when the club reached the pinnacle of football, not just in Italy but on the global stage. The legacy of this era continues to inspire future generations of players and fans, as Inter Milan remains one of the most storied and successful clubs in the world.

Chapter 11: The Decline of Grande Inter

The Beginning of the End (1967-1968)

By the mid-1960s, Inter Milan, under the guidance of Helenio Herrera, had established itself as one of the most dominant forces in European football. The *Grande Inter* era, characterized by tactical brilliance, defensive solidity, and back-to-back European Cup victories, had cemented the club's place in football history. However, as the 1960s drew to a close, the signs of decline began to emerge, signaling the beginning of the end for this legendary team.

The 1966-1967 season, which followed Inter Milan's loss to Real Madrid in the European Cup final, was a turning point. Despite still being a formidable team, Inter Milan was beginning to show signs of wear and tear. The demands of competing at the highest level year after year had taken their toll on the players, many of whom had been integral parts of the team's success since the early 1960s. The core of the squad, including key figures like Giacinto Facchetti, Luis Suárez, and Sandro Mazzola, was aging, and the physical and mental fatigue of sustained success was becoming increasingly apparent.

One of the first visible signs of decline was a dip in performance during the 1966-1967 Serie A season.

While Inter Milan remained competitive, finishing second in the league behind Juventus, the team lacked the sharpness and consistency that had defined their earlier successes. Injuries and fatigue played a significant role in this decline, as several key players struggled to maintain their previous levels of performance. The squad depth, which had been sufficient in previous years, was now being tested, and the cracks were beginning to show.

Helenio Herrera, once hailed as the tactical genius behind Inter's success, also began to face criticism. His rigid adherence to the *Catenaccio* system, which had brought so much success in the past, was now being questioned as the football landscape started to evolve. Opposing teams had begun to find ways to counter Inter's defensive style, and the tactical innovations that had once given Inter the upper hand were now being met with more sophisticated strategies from rivals. Additionally, Herrera's demanding and sometimes abrasive management style, which had driven the team to greatness, was beginning to cause friction within the squad. The intense pressure to maintain their dominance was taking a toll on the players' morale and unity.

The 1967-1968 season saw further signs of decline. Inter Milan started the season strongly, but as the campaign progressed, the team's vulnerabilities became more pronounced. Injuries continued to plague the squad, and the grueling schedule of competing in both domestic and European competitions left the players exhausted. In the European Cup, Inter Milan was eliminated in the quarter-finals by Yugoslavian club FK Partizan, a result that shocked many and highlighted the team's waning dominance on the continental stage.

In Serie A, Inter Milan once again finished second, this time behind AC Milan, who were emerging as a new force in Italian football. The loss of the league title to their city rivals was a bitter blow, underscoring the fact that Inter's grip on Italian football was slipping. The invincible aura that had surrounded the *Grande Inter* team for so many years was beginning to fade, and the club was now facing the reality of an inevitable decline.

The Final Years of Grande Inter (1968-1970)

The late 1960s were a period of transition for Inter Milan, as the club struggled to maintain the standards set during the *Grande Inter* era. The 1968-1969 season began with a sense of determination, as the team sought to reclaim its place at the top of Italian and European football. However, the challenges that had begun to surface in previous seasons continued to hinder the team's progress.

One of the key issues during this period was the aging of the squad. Many of the players who had been instrumental in Inter's success were now in the twilight of their careers. Giacinto Facchetti, Luis Suárez, and Sandro Mazzola, who had once been the pillars of the team, were no longer able to consistently perform at the highest level. The physical demands of Herrera's system, which required relentless defensive discipline and quick transitions, were becoming increasingly difficult for the aging players to execute.

The club's management faced the difficult task of balancing the need to refresh the squad with the desire to remain loyal to the players who had brought so much success. New signings were brought in, but integrating them into a team that had been so closely knit for years proved challenging. The chemistry that had defined the *Grande Inter* team was difficult to replicate, and the new players struggled to fill the shoes of their illustrious predecessors.

The 1968-1969 season was marked by inconsistency. While there were moments of brilliance, the team's performances were often uneven. Inter Milan finished fourth in Serie A, their lowest finish since Herrera's arrival. In the European Cup, the team was eliminated in the first round by

Romanian club Dinamo Bucharest, a clear indication that the team was no longer the force it once was. The early exit from Europe was particularly disappointing for a club that had been accustomed to competing for the top honors on the continent.

The frustrations of the season were compounded by growing tensions within the squad and between the players and Herrera. The once unbreakable bond between the coach and his players was beginning to fray. Herrera's intense personality and uncompromising demands, which had been tolerated during the years of success, were now sources of conflict. The players, many of whom were dealing with the physical decline that comes with age, found it increasingly difficult to meet Herrera's expectations.

The 1969-1970 season proved to be the final chapter of the *Grande Inter* era. The season began with high hopes, but it quickly became apparent that the team's best days were behind them. Injuries, poor form, and internal discord plagued the campaign. Inter Milan finished fifth in Serie A, missing out on European qualification for the first time in a decade. The club's struggles were emblematic of a team that had reached the end of its cycle.

The end of the 1969-1970 season also marked the end of Helenio Herrera's tenure as head coach of

Inter Milan. After a decade in charge, during which he had led the club to unprecedented success, Herrera parted ways with the club. His departure signaled the official end of the *Grande Inter* era. While Herrera's final years at the club were marked by decline, his legacy as one of the greatest coaches in football history remained intact. The tactical innovations he introduced and the success he brought to Inter Milan left an indelible mark on the club and the sport.

For Inter Milan, the departure of Herrera and the end of the *Grande Inter* era were both a time of reflection and a turning point. The club had achieved incredible success during the 1960s, but the challenges of maintaining that level of dominance had finally caught up with them. The decline of the *Grande Inter* team was a reminder of the cyclical nature of football, where periods of success are often followed by periods of rebuilding and renewal.

As the 1970s began, Inter Milan faced the daunting task of transitioning to a new era. The club would need to rebuild, both in terms of its squad and its identity, as it sought to recapture the glory of the *Grande Inter* years. While the end of this era was marked by challenges and decline, the legacy of the *Grande Inter* team remained a source of pride and inspiration for the club and its supporters. The achievements of the 1960s would continue to resonate throughout the history of Inter Milan, serving as a benchmark for future generations.

The decline of the *Grande Inter* era was a poignant reminder of the fragility of success in football. Even the most dominant teams eventually face challenges that bring their reign to an end. For Inter Milan, the lessons learned during this period would inform the club's future efforts to rebuild and return to the pinnacle of football. The end of the *Grande Inter* era marked the close of one of the most illustrious chapters in Inter Milan's history, but it also set the stage for new beginnings and the pursuit of future greatness.

Chapter 12: The 1970s

Inter Milan in the Early 1970s (1970-1974)

The 1970s began as a period of uncertainty and transition for Inter Milan. After the golden era of *Grande Inter* under Helenio Herrera, the club faced the daunting task of rebuilding and reestablishing itself as a dominant force in Italian and European football. The early 1970s were characterized by a series of management changes, fluctuating performances, and the challenge of moving on from the legacy of one of the greatest teams in football history.

Following the departure of Herrera in 1970, Inter Milan appointed Giovanni Invernizzi as the head coach. Invernizzi had been part of the coaching staff during the *Grande Inter* years and was seen as a steady hand who could guide the club through this transitional phase. His first task was to restore stability to a team that had struggled in the latter years of Herrera's tenure. Despite the challenges, Invernizzi made an immediate impact by leading Inter Milan to the Serie A title in the 1970-1971 season. This unexpected success, achieved with much of the old guard still in place, was a remarkable achievement and offered hope that the club could return to its former glory.

The 1970-1971 Scudetto was a bright spot in an otherwise challenging period. Invernizzi's success was built on a solid defense, with players like Giacinto Facchetti and Tarcisio Burgnich providing experience and leadership at the back. The midfield, anchored by Sandro Mazzola, continued to be a source of creativity, while the attack was led by Roberto Boninsegna, who was one of the most prolific strikers in Serie A during this time. Boninsegna's goalscoring prowess was crucial to Inter's title win, and his partnership with Mazzola was one of the highlights of the season.

However, the success of the 1970-1971 season proved to be difficult to sustain. The following seasons saw Inter Milan struggle to maintain the high standards set during the *Grande Inter* era. The team's core players were aging, and the squad lacked the depth and quality needed to compete consistently at the highest level. The departure of key players, combined with injuries and inconsistent performances, meant that Inter Milan was unable to build on its title success.

Management changes also contributed to the instability during the early 1970s. Invernizzi was replaced by Enea Masiero in 1972, and then by Giancarlo Beltrami in 1973. These frequent changes in the coaching staff reflected the club's struggles to find the right formula for success. Each coach brought different ideas and strategies, but none were able to replicate the success of Invernizzi's title-winning campaign. The constant turnover created a lack of continuity, making it difficult for the team to develop a consistent style of play.

Despite the challenges, there were moments of promise during this period. The 1971-1972 season saw Inter Milan reach the semi-finals of the European Cup, where they were narrowly defeated by Johan Cruyff's Ajax, a team that was revolutionizing European football with its "Total Football" philosophy. Although Inter Milan fell short, the performance against Ajax demonstrated that the club was still capable of competing with the best teams in Europe.

Domestically, however, the club's fortunes were mixed. The 1972-1973 season saw Inter Milan finish in a disappointing fifth place in Serie A, missing out on European qualification. The team's inconsistency was a recurring theme, as they struggled to find the balance between defense and attack that had defined their success in the 1960s. The lack of a clear tactical identity and the aging of key players continued to hinder the team's progress.

The early 1970s were a period of adjustment for Inter Milan. The club was in the process of moving on from the *Grande Inter* era, and this transition was marked by a series of ups and downs. While the 1970-1971 Scudetto was a significant achievement, it also masked the underlying issues that the club would need to address in the coming years. The frequent changes in management and the inability to build a cohesive squad meant that Inter Milan faced a challenging path ahead as they sought to rebuild and return to the top of Italian and European football.

A Decade of Instability (1974-1979)

The mid to late 1970s were marked by continued instability and struggles for Inter Milan, as the club faced significant challenges both on and off the pitch. This period was characterized by frequent changes in management, inconsistent performances, and the growing realization that the glory days of the *Grande Inter* era were now firmly in the past.

In 1974, Inter Milan appointed Luis Suárez as head coach. Suárez, a former player and one of the key figures of the *Grande Inter* team, was seen as a potential solution to the club's ongoing struggles. However, his tenure as coach was short-lived, and despite his deep understanding of the club and its history, he was unable to turn the team's fortunes around. Suárez's departure after just one season was indicative of the club's broader problems—an inability to find a stable and effective leadership.

The 1974-1975 season saw Inter Milan finish in a disappointing ninth place in Serie A, their lowest finish in years. The team's decline was evident in their performances, as they struggled to find consistency and often appeared disjointed on the pitch. The lack of a clear tactical direction and the frequent changes in coaching staff contributed to this decline. The club's once-feared defense was now vulnerable, and the attack, despite the presence of talented players like Boninsegna, was often ineffective.

Inter Milan's struggles during this period were not limited to Serie A. The club also faced challenges in European competitions. The 1974-1975 UEFA Cup campaign ended in disappointment, with Inter Milan being eliminated in the second round by Dutch side FC Twente. This early exit was a reflection of the club's inability to compete at the highest level in Europe, a far cry from the days when they had dominated the continent.

The late 1970s continued to be a time of turmoil for Inter Milan. The club went through a series of coaching changes, with Beniamino Cancian, Giulio Cappelli, and Eugenio Bersellini all taking turns at the helm. Each new coach brought different ideas and approaches, but none were able to bring the stability and success that the club so desperately needed. The constant turnover created a lack of continuity, making it difficult for the players to adapt and perform at their best.

Despite the challenges, there were some notable matches and moments during this period. One such moment came in the 1976-1977 season when Inter Milan secured a memorable victory over AC Milan in the Derby della Madonnina. The match, which ended in a 3-2 win for Inter, was a reminder of the club's enduring ability to rise to the occasion, even during difficult times. The derby win provided a brief respite from the club's struggles and gave the fans something to celebrate.

Another significant moment came in the 1977-1978 season when Inter Milan reached the final of the Coppa Italia. Although they were defeated by Napoli in the final, the run to the final was a positive sign for a club that had struggled for much of the decade. The Coppa Italia campaign provided a glimmer of hope that the club could still compete for silverware, even as they faced ongoing challenges in Serie A.

The 1978-1979 season saw yet another coaching change, with Eugenio Bersellini taking charge of the team. Bersellini's appointment marked the beginning of a more disciplined and organized approach to the team's play. His emphasis on fitness and tactical discipline helped to steady the ship, and while the results were not immediate, there were signs of improvement. Inter Milan finished fourth in Serie A that season, their best finish since 1971, and qualified for the UEFA Cup, offering a measure of optimism for the future.

The late 1970s were a difficult period for Inter Milan, marked by instability and a decline in the club's fortunes. The struggles of this decade were a stark contrast to the successes of the *Grande Inter* era, and the club found itself in a prolonged period of transition. The frequent changes in management, the aging of key players, and the inability to build a cohesive and competitive squad all contributed to the challenges faced during this time.

As the 1970s came to a close, Inter Milan was a club in search of a new identity. The decade had been one of instability and inconsistency, but it had also been a period of learning and adaptation. The club's management and supporters knew that rebuilding would take time, but there was a growing sense that with the right leadership and a renewed focus, Inter Milan could once again return to the top of Italian and European football.

The experiences of the 1970s would ultimately shape the club's approach in the years to come. The lessons learned from this decade of struggle would inform the decisions made in the 1980s, as Inter Milan sought to reclaim its place among the elite. While the 1970s were a challenging period, they also set the stage for a new era of growth and development, as the club worked to rebuild and renew itself for the future.

Chapter 13: The Late 1970s to Early 1980s

The Road to Recovery (1979-1982)

As the 1970s drew to a close, Inter Milan found itself at a crossroads. The club had endured a decade of instability, marked by frequent changes in management, inconsistent performances, and a lack of silverware. However, there were signs that the club was beginning to find its footing again, with steps being taken to restore competitiveness and lay the groundwork for a new era of success.

One of the pivotal moments in Inter Milan's road to recovery came with the appointment of Eugenio Bersellini as head coach in 1977. Bersellini, known for his disciplined and methodical approach to coaching, was tasked with bringing stability to the team and rebuilding a squad capable of challenging for honors. His emphasis on fitness, tactical organization, and hard work resonated with the players, and over time, these principles began to bear fruit.

The 1979-1980 season marked the beginning of Inter Milan's resurgence under Bersellini. The club made several key signings that would prove instrumental in their return to competitiveness. One of the most significant acquisitions was that of Alessandro Altobelli, a prolific striker who would become one of the club's most important players during this period. Altobelli's ability to score goals consistently made him a crucial asset for Inter, and he quickly established himself as a fan favorite.

Another key signing was midfielder Gabriele Oriali, who brought tenacity and work rate to the team. Oriali's presence in the midfield provided the balance needed to support both the defense and the attack, making him an indispensable part of Bersellini's system. These signings, along with the development of existing talents like Giuseppe Baresi and the emerging Franco Causio, helped to strengthen the squad and create a more cohesive unit.

The 1979-1980 Serie A season saw Inter Milan emerge as genuine title contenders. Bersellini's tactical approach, which focused on a strong defense and efficient counter-attacking play, proved effective in a league known for its tactical battles. Inter's defense, led by Baresi and the experienced Graziano Bini, was one of the best in the league, while Altobelli's goalscoring exploits ensured that the team remained competitive in every match.

Inter Milan's efforts culminated in the club winning the Serie A title in 1980, their first Scudetto in nearly a decade. The title win was a significant achievement for the club and a testament to the work done by Bersellini and his players. The victory was not just a return to the top of Italian football, but also a statement that Inter Milan was once again a force to be reckoned with. The Scudetto win was celebrated with great enthusiasm by the club's supporters, who had endured years of frustration and disappointment.

The success of the 1979-1980 season laid the foundation for further achievements in the early 1980s. The club continued to build on its success by making strategic signings and nurturing young talent. In the summer of 1980, Inter Milan signed midfielder Hansi Müller, a German international who brought creativity and vision to the midfield. Müller's arrival added a new dimension to the team's play, as his passing and playmaking abilities complemented the more industrious players like Oriali.

Inter Milan also saw the emergence of talented young players from their youth academy, including the promising defender Riccardo Ferri. Ferri, who would go on to become one of the club's stalwarts, was gradually integrated into the first team, providing fresh energy and defensive solidity. The club's focus on developing young talent, combined with astute signings, helped to ensure that the team remained competitive in both domestic and European competitions.

The early 1980s saw Inter Milan consistently finish near the top of Serie A, although they were unable to replicate the title-winning success of 1980. The team also made notable progress in European competitions, reaching the semi-finals of the UEFA Cup in 1981. Although they were eventually eliminated by Real Madrid, the campaign highlighted the club's growing stature on the European stage and provided valuable experience for the players.

The period from 1979 to 1982 was one of recovery and rebuilding for Inter Milan. The steps taken during these years, including key signings, the development of young talent, and the establishment of a more disciplined and organized team, set the stage for the club's continued competitiveness in the years to come. The return to success in Serie A and the progress made in Europe demonstrated that Inter Milan was once again on the right path, with the potential to achieve even greater things in the future.

Inter Milan in Transition (1982-1985)

The early 1980s were a time of transition for Inter Milan, as the club continued to navigate the challenges of maintaining its competitiveness in a rapidly evolving football landscape. While the team had made significant strides in the late 1970s and early 1980s, the years that followed were marked by further developments, management changes, and the ongoing quest to build a squad capable of consistently challenging for top honors.

Following the success of the 1979-1980 Scudetto, Eugenio Bersellini remained at the helm of the club, guiding Inter Milan through a period of relative stability. However, as the 1980s progressed, it became clear that the team needed to evolve to keep pace with the changing dynamics of Serie A and European football. The physical demands of the game were increasing, and clubs were investing heavily in both domestic and international talent to strengthen their squads.

In 1982, Inter Milan made a significant move by appointing Rino Marchesi as head coach. Marchesi, a former player with experience in managing several Italian clubs, was brought in to bring a fresh perspective to the team. His appointment was part of a broader effort to modernize the club's approach and build a team that could compete at the highest level both in Italy and in Europe. Marchesi's arrival signaled the beginning of a new phase in Inter Milan's transition, as the club sought to balance its traditional strengths with a more dynamic and forward-thinking style of play.

One of the key challenges during this period was the need to refresh the squad with new talent while maintaining the core of experienced players who had been instrumental in the club's recent successes. Inter Milan continued to invest in the transfer market, bringing in players who could add quality and depth to the team. In 1982, the club signed Evaristo Beccalossi, a creative midfielder known for his dribbling skills and vision. Beccalossi's ability to unlock defenses with his passing and movement made him a valuable addition to the squad.

Another significant signing was that of Walter Zenga, a talented goalkeeper who would go on to become one of the most iconic figures in Inter Milan's history. Zenga's arrival in 1982 marked the beginning of a long and successful career at the club, where he would establish himself as one of the best goalkeepers in the world. His leadership and shot-stopping abilities provided stability at the back, giving the team confidence in their defensive solidity.

Despite these promising additions, the early 1980s were also marked by challenges. The team struggled with consistency, often performing well in individual matches but failing to sustain a high level of play over the course of a season. Injuries to key players and the difficulty of integrating new signings into the squad contributed to this inconsistency. While Inter Milan remained competitive in Serie A, finishing in the top half of the table, they were unable to mount a serious challenge for the Scudetto during this period.

In European competitions, Inter Milan faced mixed fortunes. The club participated in the UEFA Cup and the European Cup Winners' Cup, but they were unable to progress beyond the quarter-finals in either competition. The team's performances in Europe highlighted the need for further strengthening and tactical refinement if they were to compete with the top clubs on the continent.

The 1983-1984 season saw further changes, as Marchesi was replaced by Ilario Castagner as head coach. Castagner, known for his pragmatic approach and emphasis on defensive organization, was tasked with stabilizing the team and improving their performances in both domestic and European competitions. However, his tenure was short-lived, and despite some promising results, the team continued to struggle with inconsistency.

The 1984-1985 season marked another period of transition for Inter Milan. The club brought in several new players, including Austrian forward Karl-Heinz Rummenigge, who was one of the most highly regarded strikers in Europe at the time. Rummenigge's arrival was a statement of intent from the club, signaling their ambition to compete at the highest level. His experience, goal-scoring ability, and leadership were seen as crucial assets for a team looking to return to the summit of Italian football.

Despite the high-profile signings, the 1984-1985 season was marked by further challenges. Inter Milan finished third in Serie A, a respectable position but still short of the club's ambitions. The team also made progress in the UEFA Cup, reaching the semi-finals before being eliminated by Real Madrid. While the season showed signs of promise, it was clear that Inter Milan was still in the process of finding the right balance and identity as they transitioned into a new era.

The early 1980s were a time of transition and rebuilding for Inter Milan. The club was working to restore its competitiveness in a rapidly changing football landscape, making key signings and adjustments to their approach. While the team faced challenges and inconsistencies during this period, the foundations were being laid for future success. The steps taken during these years, including the acquisition of talented players and the development of a more modern style of play, would eventually bear fruit as Inter Milan continued its journey towards reclaiming its place among the elite of Italian and European football.

Chapter 14: The Trapattoni Era

The Arrival of Giovanni Trapattoni (1986)

By the mid-1980s, Inter Milan was a club in search of renewed glory. The previous decade had been marked by periods of instability and transition, and while the team had shown flashes of promise, consistent success had eluded them. The club's management, led by president Ernesto Pellegrini, recognized the need for a strong, experienced leader who could instill discipline, tactical acumen, and a winning mentality in the squad. This led to the appointment of Giovanni Trapattoni as head coach in 1986, a decision that would prove to be a turning point in the club's history.

Giovanni Trapattoni was already a highly respected figure in Italian football by the time he arrived at Inter Milan. His coaching career had begun at AC Milan, where he had been a player, but it was at Juventus that he truly made his mark. During his time with Juventus, Trapattoni won numerous domestic and international titles, establishing himself as one of the most successful and tactically astute managers in Europe. His teams were known for their discipline, organization, and ability to grind out results, qualities that earned him a reputation as a master strategist.

The circumstances surrounding Trapattoni's appointment at Inter Milan were shaped by the club's desire to break the dominance of their rivals, AC Milan and Juventus, who had been the dominant forces in Serie A during the early 1980s. Inter Milan had not won a league title since 1980, and there was a growing sense of urgency to restore the club to its former glory. Pellegrini saw Trapattoni as the ideal candidate to lead this revival, believing that his experience, tactical knowledge, and winning mentality would be exactly what Inter Milan needed to return to the top.

Trapattoni's arrival was met with a mixture of excitement and cautious optimism. Fans and pundits alike were aware of his impressive track record, but they also understood the challenges he faced at Inter Milan. The squad was talented but had underperformed in recent years, and there were concerns about the team's mental toughness and ability to compete consistently at the highest level. Trapattoni's task was to mold this group of players into a cohesive, disciplined unit capable of challenging for the Scudetto.

One of the first things Trapattoni did upon taking charge was to instill a sense of discipline and organization within the team. He was known for his meticulous approach to tactics, and he wasted no time in implementing a system that emphasized defensive solidity, tactical awareness, and teamwork. Trapattoni's teams were built on a strong defensive foundation, and at Inter Milan, he placed great importance on the backline, ensuring that the team was difficult to break down and could withstand pressure from even the most potent attacks.

To achieve this, Trapattoni relied on experienced defenders like Riccardo Ferri and Giuseppe Bergomi, who became the bedrock of Inter's defense. Ferri, known for his physicality and ability to read the game, was a key figure in Trapattoni's plans, while Bergomi's leadership and consistency made him an indispensable part of the team. Trapattoni also focused on developing a midfield that could control the tempo of games and support both the defense and the attack. Players like Gianfranco Matteoli and Lothar Matthäus, a German international who arrived in 1988, played crucial roles in Trapattoni's system.

Trapattoni's emphasis on discipline and organization paid off quickly. Inter Milan became known for their ability to win matches by narrow margins, often grinding out results through sheer determination and tactical acumen. The team's performances in the 1986-1987 and 1987-1988 seasons showed marked improvement, with Inter Milan consistently finishing in the top four of Serie A and qualifying for European competitions. While the team was still a work in progress, it was clear that Trapattoni was building a squad capable of challenging for major honors.

The 1989 Scudetto and Its Impact

The 1988-1989 season would prove to be the crowning achievement of Giovanni Trapattoni's time at Inter Milan. After two seasons of steady progress, Trapattoni had molded a team that was not only tactically disciplined but also possessed the mental toughness and winning mentality needed to compete at the highest level. The key to this transformation was the combination of experienced Italian players and a core of talented foreign stars, most notably the German trio of Lothar Matthäus, Andreas Brehme, and Jürgen Klinsmann, who were instrumental in the team's success.

The 1988-1989 Serie A campaign was one of the most dominant in Italian football history. From the very start of the season, Inter Milan set the pace, quickly establishing themselves as the team to beat. Trapattoni's tactical approach, which emphasized a solid defense, quick transitions, and clinical finishing, proved highly effective. The team went on an incredible run, winning 26 of their 34 matches and losing only two. They finished the season with 58 points, a record at the time under the two-point-per-win system, and a remarkable 11 points clear of second-placed Napoli.

Central to this success was Lothar Matthäus, who had joined Inter Milan in 1988 from Bayern Munich. Matthäus was the driving force in midfield, combining technical ability with physical power and an unyielding will to win. His presence added a new dimension to Inter's play, as he was capable of both breaking up opposition attacks and launching his team forward with dynamic runs and pinpoint passes. Matthäus also contributed crucial goals, including several match-winners, that kept Inter at the top of the table.

Andreas Brehme, another key signing from Germany, brought versatility and reliability to the team. Brehme, who could play as both a left-back and a left midfielder, was known for his precise crossing, powerful shots, and dead-ball expertise. His ability to contribute both defensively and offensively made him an invaluable asset in Trapattoni's system, and his understanding with Matthäus added to the team's overall cohesion.

Up front, Jürgen Klinsmann provided the finishing touch. The German striker, who joined Inter in 1989, quickly adapted to Serie A and became one of the league's most feared forwards. Klinsmann's pace, movement, and clinical finishing made him a constant threat to opposition defenses, and his partnership with Aldo Serena, the Italian striker who won the league's top scorer award that season, was a key factor in Inter's success. Serena's physical presence and ability to hold up the ball complemented Klinsmann's more direct style, creating a well-balanced and potent attack.

Defensively, Inter Milan was almost impenetrable. The backline, marshaled by Ferri and Bergomi, conceded just 19 goals all season, the fewest in the league. Goalkeeper Walter Zenga, who had become one of the best in the world, was in outstanding form, consistently producing crucial saves to keep Inter in control of matches. The combination of a solid defense, a dynamic midfield, and a lethal attack made Inter Milan the most complete team in Italy that season.

The 1989 Scudetto was more than just a league title; it was a statement of Inter Milan's return to the pinnacle of Italian football. The victory ended a nine-year wait for the Scudetto and brought immense joy to the club's supporters, who had longed for a return to the glory days of the *Grande Inter* era. The title win also solidified Giovanni Trapattoni's legacy as one of the greatest managers in the club's history, as he had successfully restored Inter Milan to its rightful place among the elite.

The impact of the 1989 Scudetto extended beyond the immediate celebration. It marked the beginning of a new era of competitiveness for Inter Milan, as the club re-established itself as a major force in both domestic and European football. The success of the 1988-1989 season served as a foundation for the club's future endeavors, both on and off the pitch. The team's success attracted more top players to the club, and Inter Milan's reputation as a club capable of winning major trophies was reinforced.

The 1989 Scudetto also had a lasting impact on the culture and identity of Inter Milan. The triumph was seen as a vindication of the club's decision to bring in foreign talent and blend it with the best of Italian football. This approach would continue to define Inter Milan's strategy in the years to come, as the club sought to compete with the best teams in Europe. The success of the German contingent, in particular, highlighted the importance of international players in achieving success, a philosophy that would remain central to Inter Milan's identity.

For the players who were part of the 1989 Scudetto-winning team, the achievement was a career-defining moment. Lothar Matthäus, Andreas

Brehme, and Jürgen Klinsmann all went on to achieve further success with their national team, winning the 1990 FIFA World Cup with West Germany. Their contributions to Inter Milan's success were recognized and celebrated by the club's supporters, who continue to regard them as legends.

The 1989 Scudetto remains one of the most cherished titles in Inter Milan's history. It was a triumph that symbolized the club's resilience, ambition, and ability to adapt to changing circumstances. The success of the Trapattoni era laid the groundwork for future successes and reinforced Inter Milan's status as one of the giants of Italian and European football. The lessons learned and the foundations built during this period would continue to influence the club's approach in the years to come, as Inter Milan continued its pursuit of greatness.

Chapter 15: The 1990s

The Early 1990s: Near Misses (1990-1995)

The 1990s began with high expectations for Inter Milan, following the success of the late 1980s under Giovanni Trapattoni. The club had won the Serie A title in 1989, and with a strong squad featuring some of the best players in Europe, the hope was that Inter could build on this success and establish a new era of dominance. However, the early 1990s would prove to be a period of frustration and near misses, as the club struggled to convert its potential into more league titles.

After the 1989 Scudetto, Inter Milan entered the 1990-1991 season as one of the favorites for the title. The team, still managed by Trapattoni, boasted a solid defense led by Giuseppe Bergomi and Riccardo Ferri, a dynamic midfield with Lothar Matthäus and Nicola Berti, and a potent attack featuring Jürgen Klinsmann and Aldo Serena. Despite these strengths, Inter found it difficult to maintain consistency throughout the season. Key injuries, including one to Matthäus, disrupted the team's rhythm, and while Inter remained competitive, they ultimately finished in third place, behind Sampdoria and AC Milan.

The following seasons saw a continuation of this pattern of near misses. In the 1991-1992 season, Trapattoni left the club to return to Juventus, and Inter appointed Corrado Orrico as his replacement. Orrico's tenure was short-lived, as his attempts to implement a more defensive style of play were met with resistance from both players and fans. The team struggled under Orrico, and he was replaced midway through the season by Luis Suárez, a former Inter star and coach. Despite the change, Inter finished a disappointing eighth in Serie A, well off the pace of the title challengers.

The 1992-1993 season brought further frustration. Inter Milan made a series of high-profile signings, including Dutch forward Dennis Bergkamp and German midfielder Matthias Sammer, in an effort to revitalize the squad. Bergkamp, a highly skilled and creative player, was seen as the successor to Matthäus, who had left the club to join Bayern Munich. However, while Bergkamp showed flashes of brilliance, the team as a whole struggled to find cohesion. Inter finished in second place in Serie A, but they were a distant 10 points behind the champions, AC Milan. The inability to close the gap on their city rivals highlighted the ongoing challenges facing the club.

The 1993-1994 season saw the arrival of Giampiero Marini as head coach, replacing Osvaldo Bagnoli, who had been brought in the previous year. Marini, a former Inter midfielder, was tasked with reinvigorating the team, but despite his best efforts, the season ended in disappointment. Inter finished in 13th place in Serie A, just one point above the relegation zone. The club's struggles were compounded by a lack of stability in the squad, with frequent changes in personnel and tactics. The near-misses of the early 1990s were taking their toll, as the club searched for a winning formula.

Despite these struggles, there were moments of hope and promise during this period. The team's performances in European competitions, particularly the UEFA Cup, provided some consolation to the fans. However, the inability to secure another Serie A title during the early 1990s left a lingering sense of unfulfilled potential. The near-misses in the league were a source of frustration, as Inter Milan repeatedly fell short in their pursuit of domestic success.

European Success in the UEFA Cup (1990-1995)

While Inter Milan struggled to achieve consistent success in Serie A during the early 1990s, the club found solace in European competitions, particularly the UEFA Cup. The UEFA Cup, a prestigious tournament that featured some of the best teams from across Europe, became a stage where Inter Milan could showcase their talents and reclaim some of the glory that had eluded them domestically.

The 1990-1991 UEFA Cup campaign was a significant one for Inter Milan. The team, still managed by Giovanni Trapattoni, approached the tournament with determination and focus. After navigating the early rounds, Inter faced Italian rivals Atalanta in the quarter-finals. In a closely contested tie, Inter emerged victorious, setting up a semi-final clash with Sporting CP of Portugal. The semi-final was a tense affair, but Inter's experience and tactical discipline saw them through to the final, where they would face AS Roma in an all-Italian showdown.

The UEFA Cup final, played over two legs, was a hard-fought battle between two evenly matched teams. In the first leg at the Stadio Giuseppe Meazza, Inter secured a 2-0 victory, with goals from Matthäus and Berti. The second leg, played at the Stadio Olimpico in Rome, saw Roma win 1-0, but it was not enough to overturn Inter's advantage. Inter Milan won the UEFA Cup 2-1 on aggregate, securing their first major European trophy since the *Grande Inter* era. The victory was a testament to the team's resilience and provided a much-needed boost after the disappointment of their domestic campaign.

The success in the UEFA Cup continued in the following seasons. In the 1993-1994 UEFA Cup, Inter Milan once again reached the final, this time under the management of Giampiero Marini. The team's journey to the final was marked by impressive performances, including a memorable victory over Borussia Dortmund in the semi-finals. The final saw Inter face Austria Salzburg, a surprise finalist from Austria. Inter won the first leg 1-0 in Salzburg, thanks to a goal from Nicola Berti, and completed the job with a 1-0 win in the second leg at the San Siro, with Wim Jonk scoring the decisive goal. Inter Milan won the UEFA Cup 2-0 on aggregate, securing their second European trophy in four years.

These UEFA Cup victories were significant for several reasons. First and foremost, they demonstrated that Inter Milan was still capable of competing at the highest level in European football, even as they struggled in Serie A. The triumphs in Europe also helped to restore some of the club's prestige and provided a platform for players like Matthäus, Berti, and Bergomi to shine on the continental stage. The UEFA Cup successes were a source of pride for the fans, who had endured years of frustration and near misses in the league.

However, the UEFA Cup victories also highlighted the contrast between Inter's performances in Europe and their struggles in domestic competitions. While the team was able to achieve success in the knockout format of the UEFA Cup, where tactical discipline and experience were crucial, they found it more difficult to maintain consistency over the course of a long Serie A season. The near-misses in the league, combined with the successes in Europe, created a sense of duality in the club's identity during the early 1990s.

Ronaldo's Arrival and the Mid-1990s (1995-1997)

The mid-1990s marked a period of significant change for Inter Milan, as the club sought to rebuild and reestablish itself as a dominant force in Italian football. One of the most important developments during this period was the arrival of Brazilian superstar Ronaldo, who would become one of the most iconic players in the club's history.

In 1995, Inter Milan was taken over by Massimo Moratti, the son of Angelo Moratti, who had been the president during the *Grande Inter* era. The younger Moratti shared his father's passion for the club and was determined to restore Inter to its former glory. To achieve this, Moratti embarked on an ambitious project to revamp the squad, bringing in top talent from around the world. One of his most significant moves was the signing of Ronaldo from Barcelona in 1997 for a then-world record transfer fee.

Ronaldo, known as "O Fenômeno" (The Phenomenon), was widely regarded as the best player in the world at the time. His combination of speed, strength, technical ability, and clinical finishing made him a nightmare for defenders and a dream signing for any club. Ronaldo's arrival at Inter Milan sent shockwaves through the football world and signaled the club's intent to compete with the best teams in Europe.

Ronaldo's impact on Inter Milan was immediate and profound. In his first season with the club (1997-1998), he scored 25 goals in Serie A, finishing as the league's second-highest scorer. His performances were nothing short of sensational, as he dazzled fans and opponents alike with his incredible dribbling, powerful shots, and ability to score from seemingly impossible situations. Ronaldo quickly became the face of Inter Milan, embodying the club's ambition and desire to return to the top.

Ronaldo's presence also had a positive effect on the rest of the squad. Players like Iván Zamorano, Javier Zanetti, and Youri Djorkaeff, who had already been important contributors, found new motivation and confidence playing alongside the Brazilian superstar. The team's attacking play became more dynamic and unpredictable, with Ronaldo leading the charge.

Despite Ronaldo's brilliance, Inter Milan's domestic campaign in 1997-1998 was marked by frustration and controversy. The team finished second in Serie A, just five points behind Juventus, in a season that was marred by several contentious refereeing decisions. The most infamous incident occurred in a crucial match against Juventus, where a controversial non-call on a penalty for Inter sparked outrage among the club's fans and players. The sense of injustice and the near-miss in the title race added to the pressure on the team, as they sought to break Juventus' stranglehold on the Scudetto.

The 1998 UEFA Cup Win

While the 1997-1998 Serie A campaign ended in disappointment, Inter Milan found redemption in the UEFA Cup. The team's performances in Europe during the 1997-1998 season were a continuation of their strong tradition in the competition, and the UEFA Cup provided an opportunity to secure a major trophy in a season that had promised so much.

Inter Milan's journey to the 1998 UEFA Cup final was marked by several impressive performances. The team navigated through the early rounds with relative ease, before facing French side Strasbourg in the quarter-finals. After losing the first leg 2-0 away, Inter produced a stunning comeback in the second leg, winning 3-0 at the San Siro to advance to the semi-finals. In the semi-finals, Inter faced Spartak Moscow, and after a hard-fought 2-1 victory in the first leg, they secured a 2-1 win in the return leg to book their place in the final.

The final, held on May 6, 1998, at the Parc des Princes in Paris, was an all-Italian affair, as Inter Milan faced Lazio. Lazio, led by coach Sven-Göran Eriksson, had been one of the top teams in Serie A and were determined to win their first major European trophy. However, Inter Milan, driven by the desire to make amends for their domestic disappointment, produced one of their best performances of the season.

Inter took the lead early in the match, with Zamorano scoring after just five minutes. The goal set the tone for the rest of the match, as Inter dominated proceedings with their aggressive pressing and quick transitions. Ronaldo, who had been in scintillating form throughout the tournament, doubled Inter's lead in the 60th minute with a brilliant solo effort, dribbling past the Lazio defense before slotting the ball into the net. Zanetti added a third goal late in the match with a powerful long-range strike, sealing a comprehensive 3-0 victory for Inter Milan.

The 1998 UEFA Cup win was a significant achievement for Inter Milan. It was the club's third UEFA Cup triumph, making them one of the most successful teams in the history of the competition. The victory was also a testament to the team's resilience and ability to perform on the big stage, even after the disappointment of the Serie A campaign. For Ronaldo, the UEFA Cup win was his first major trophy with Inter Milan and a fitting reward for his incredible performances throughout the season.

The significance of the 1998 UEFA Cup win extended beyond the immediate celebration. It marked the culmination of a period of rebuilding and transition for Inter Milan, as the club had worked to reestablish itself as a major force in European football. The triumph also reinforced the club's reputation as a team that could compete with the best, both domestically and internationally.

For Massimo Moratti, the victory was a validation of his investment and vision for the club. The signing of Ronaldo and the success in the UEFA Cup demonstrated that Inter Milan was once again a club capable of attracting the best talent and competing for major honors. The 1998 UEFA Cup win remains one of the most cherished moments in the club's history, a symbol of the team's resilience, ambition, and commitment to excellence.

As the 1990s came to a close, Inter Milan faced new challenges and opportunities. The successes and near-misses of the decade had shaped the club's identity and laid the groundwork for future endeavors. The arrival of Ronaldo and the UEFA Cup triumph of 1998 were high points in a decade that had seen both triumph and frustration. The lessons learned during this period would continue to influence the club's approach in the years to come, as Inter Milan pursued its goal of returning to the pinnacle of Italian and European football.

Chapter 16: The Moratti Era

Massimo Moratti's Vision (1995-2000)

The mid-1990s marked the beginning of a new chapter in the history of Inter Milan with the arrival of Massimo Moratti as the club's president. Moratti, the son of Angelo Moratti, who had presided over the *Grande Inter* era of the 1960s, took over the reins of the club in 1995 with a clear vision: to restore Inter Milan to its former glory and reestablish the club as a dominant force in both Italian and European football.

Massimo Moratti's deep emotional connection to Inter Milan was evident from the outset. His father's legacy loomed large, and Massimo was determined to build a team that could replicate the success of the 1960s, when Inter Milan had won back-to-back European Cups and numerous domestic titles. To achieve this, Moratti was prepared to invest heavily in the squad, bringing in top talent from around the world to compete with the best.

One of Moratti's first major moves was the signing of Paul Ince, the dynamic English midfielder from Manchester United. Ince's arrival in 1995 signaled Moratti's intent to build a team that could compete with the elite clubs in Europe. Ince brought experience, leadership, and a winning mentality to the squad, and his presence in the midfield was meant to be the foundation of the new Inter Milan. However, while Ince became a fan favorite for his tenacity and passion, the team's overall performances remained inconsistent.

Moratti's ambition and willingness to spend big were further demonstrated in 1997 when he broke the world transfer record to bring Brazilian superstar Ronaldo to Inter Milan from Barcelona. Ronaldo, widely regarded as the best player in the world at the time, was a game-changer. His arrival generated immense excitement among the fans and raised the club's profile globally. Ronaldo's combination of pace, power, and skill made him a nightmare for defenders and a joy to watch for supporters. His signing was a clear statement that Inter Milan was serious about challenging for major honors.

However, building a competitive team proved to be more challenging than Moratti had anticipated. Despite the high-profile signings, including Ronaldo, Inter struggled to find consistency in Serie A. The club's performances were often erratic, with moments of brilliance followed by disappointing results. The constant pressure to deliver results, coupled with the expectations placed on the team due to the significant investments, created a challenging environment for both players and coaches.

Moratti's passion for the club sometimes led to impulsive decisions, particularly in the hiring and firing of coaches. The late 1990s saw a series of managerial changes, with coaches struggling to implement their ideas and achieve the desired results. The instability in the dugout made it difficult for the team to build cohesion and develop a consistent style of play. Coaches like Roy Hodgson, Luigi Simoni, and Mircea Lucescu all had brief stints in charge, with varying degrees of success, but none were able to fully capitalize on the talent within the squad.

The pressure to succeed also led to tensions within the team. The expectations placed on star players like Ronaldo were immense, and while he delivered on many occasions, injuries and the burden of carrying the team at times took their toll. The squad lacked the depth and balance needed to compete across all fronts, and despite the talent available, Inter Milan often fell short in the league.

Moratti's investments extended beyond the playing squad. He also sought to modernize the club's infrastructure, including improvements to the training facilities and the San Siro stadium. His vision was not just about short-term success but about building a sustainable foundation for the future. However, the immediate focus remained on delivering results on the pitch, and the lack of a coherent long-term strategy made it difficult to achieve the desired outcomes.

The Late 1990s Struggles and Revival (1997-2000)

The late 1990s were a tumultuous period for Inter Milan, marked by both struggles and signs of revival. Despite the significant investments made by Massimo Moratti, the club found it difficult to challenge for the Serie A title consistently. The 1997-1998 season, which had begun with such promise following the arrival of Ronaldo, ended in disappointment, with Inter finishing second in the league, just behind Juventus. The sense of frustration was compounded by controversial refereeing decisions, particularly in a crucial match against Juventus, which many believed had cost Inter the title.

The disappointment in Serie A was offset by success in the UEFA Cup, where Inter Milan triumphed, defeating Lazio 3-0 in the final to secure the trophy. The victory was a significant achievement and provided some consolation for the club and its supporters. Ronaldo was instrumental in this success, and his performances in Europe reinforced his status as one of the world's best players.

However, the UEFA Cup win also highlighted the contrast between Inter's performances in Europe and their struggles in domestic competitions.

The 1998-1999 season saw a continuation of these challenges. Injuries to key players, including Ronaldo, who suffered a serious knee injury that would keep him out for an extended period, severely hampered the team's chances. The absence of their talisman, combined with ongoing instability in the coaching setup, made it difficult for Inter to mount a serious title challenge. The club finished a disappointing eighth in Serie A, missing out on European qualification altogether. The season was marked by further managerial changes, with Luciano Castellini, Mircea Lucescu, and Roy Hodgson all taking turns at the helm, but none could turn the tide.

The 1999-2000 season brought renewed hope with the appointment of Marcello Lippi as head coach. Lippi, who had enjoyed great success with Juventus, was seen as the man to bring stability and a winning mentality to Inter Milan. His arrival was part of a broader effort by Moratti to revive the club's fortunes, and Lippi's experience and tactical acumen were expected to make an immediate impact.

Lippi's tenure got off to a promising start, with Inter showing signs of improvement in both domestic and European competitions. The club made it to the Coppa Italia final, where they were narrowly defeated by Lazio, and also finished fourth in Serie A, securing a place in the Champions League qualifiers. However, the inconsistency that had plagued the team in previous years remained a problem. Injuries continued to disrupt the squad, and while there were moments of brilliance, particularly from players like Christian Vieri, who had joined the club in 1999, Inter struggled to find the consistency needed to challenge for the top honors.

The late 1990s were a period of highs and lows for Inter Milan. The club's struggles in Serie A were a source of frustration for Moratti and the fans, but there were also moments of optimism, particularly in European competitions. The UEFA Cup victory in 1998 and the appointment of Lippi in 1999 provided hope that the club was on the right track, but the ongoing challenges, including injuries, instability in the coaching setup, and the pressure to deliver immediate results, made it difficult to achieve sustained success.

The Impact of Calciopoli on Inter Milan (2006)

The mid-2000s brought about one of the most significant events in the history of Italian football: the Calciopoli scandal. This match-fixing scandal, which came to light in 2006, implicated several of Italy's top clubs, including Juventus, AC Milan, Fiorentina, and Lazio. The scandal had far-reaching consequences for Italian football and played a pivotal role in reshaping the landscape of Serie A. For Inter Milan, Calciopoli marked a turning point, as the club emerged as one of the biggest beneficiaries of the fallout.

Calciopoli involved the manipulation of referee appointments and match outcomes by several top clubs, aimed at gaining favorable results in Serie A. The scandal shocked the football world and led to widespread condemnation and legal action. Juventus, the most prominent club involved, was hit hardest, with the club being stripped of their 2005 and 2006 Serie A titles and relegated to Serie B. AC Milan, Fiorentina, and Lazio also faced penalties, including point deductions and exclusion from European competitions.

Inter Milan, which had not been implicated in the scandal, was awarded the 2005-2006 Serie A title following Juventus' relegation and the annulment of their title. While some questioned the legitimacy of the title, given the circumstances under which it was awarded, it marked the beginning of a period of dominance for Inter Milan in Italian football.

The impact of Calciopoli on Inter Milan was profound. With several of their main rivals weakened by the scandal, Inter found themselves in a strong position to assert their dominance in Serie A. Massimo Moratti, who had endured years of frustration and near misses, saw this as an opportunity to finally establish Inter Milan as the top club in Italy. The club's leadership, led by Moratti and coach Roberto Mancini, capitalized on the situation by strengthening the squad and building a team capable of sustaining success over multiple seasons.

One of the key factors in Inter Milan's post-Calciopoli success was the strength of their squad. In the years leading up to 2006, Moratti had continued to invest in top talent, and the club had built a team with a solid defensive foundation, a dynamic midfield, and a potent attack. Players like Javier Zanetti, Marco Materazzi, Dejan Stanković, and Zlatan Ibrahimović were central to Inter's success, providing the quality and experience needed to dominate Serie A.

The 2006-2007 season saw Inter Milan win the Serie A title in emphatic fashion, finishing with 97 points,

22 points ahead of second-placed Roma. The team's performances were marked by consistency, discipline, and a winning mentality that had been lacking in previous years. The title win was the first of five consecutive Scudetti for Inter Milan, as the club established itself as the undisputed powerhouse in Italian football.

Calciopoli also had a significant impact on the perception of Inter Milan, both within Italy and internationally. The scandal had tarnished the reputation of many of their rivals, and Inter's success in the aftermath of Calciopoli was seen by some as a vindication of the club's integrity and commitment to fair play. The club's dominance in Serie A during this period was a source of pride for the fans, who had endured years of frustration and disappointment.

The impact of Calciopoli on Inter Milan extended beyond the immediate success in Serie A. The scandal reshaped the competitive landscape of Italian football, weakening some of the club's main rivals and allowing Inter to build a period of sustained dominance. The lessons learned during the struggles of the 1990s and early 2000s, combined with the opportunity presented by Calciopoli, enabled Inter Milan to finally achieve the success that Massimo Moratti had long sought.

For Moratti, the success of the post-Calciopoli era was the culmination of years of investment, passion, and perseverance. The club's dominance in Serie A, combined with their success in European competitions, including the historic treble in 2010, cemented his legacy as one of the most influential figures in the history of Inter Milan. The impact of Calciopoli on the club's fortunes cannot be understated, as it provided the platform for Inter Milan to achieve unprecedented success and reestablish themselves as one of the top clubs in Europe.

The Moratti era, shaped by the vision, challenges, and triumphs of Massimo Moratti, was a defining period in the history of Inter Milan. From the struggles and near misses of the late 1990s to the dominance of the post-Calciopoli era, the club's journey was marked by a relentless pursuit of success. The impact of Calciopoli, and the way Inter Milan capitalized on the opportunities it presented, played a crucial role in the club's revival and eventual return to the pinnacle of Italian and European football.

Chapter 17: The 2000s

Inter's Domestic Dominance Begins (2006-2008)

The mid-2000s marked a significant shift in the landscape of Italian football, as Inter Milan began a period of domestic dominance that would define the club for years to come. This era, which started in the aftermath of the Calciopoli scandal, saw Inter rise to the pinnacle of Serie A, establishing themselves as the undisputed force in Italian football.

Following the impact of Calciopoli in 2006, Inter Milan found themselves in a strong position to capitalize on the weakened state of their rivals, particularly Juventus and AC Milan, who were both heavily penalized by the scandal. With Juventus relegated to Serie B and AC Milan starting the 2006-2007 season with a significant points deduction, Inter's path to success in Serie A was cleared. The club, under the leadership of Massimo Moratti and coach Roberto Mancini, seized this opportunity with both hands.

The 2006-2007 Serie A season was a landmark campaign for Inter Milan. The team, bolstered by a talented squad and buoyed by the opportunity to dominate the league, went on an extraordinary run. Inter set a new Serie A record by winning 17 consecutive matches, showcasing their superiority over the rest of the competition. The team's consistency, depth, and tactical discipline were unmatched, and they finished the season with 97 points, 22 points ahead of second-placed Roma. This title win was particularly sweet for the club and its supporters, as it marked Inter's first outright Scudetto in nearly two decades, following the controversial title win in 2006.

Inter's dominance was built on a solid foundation across the pitch. The defense, marshaled by the ever-reliable Javier Zanetti and the towering presence of Marco Materazzi, was nearly impenetrable. In midfield, players like Dejan Stanković, Patrick Vieira, and Esteban Cambiasso provided both creativity and grit, while the attack, led by Zlatan Ibrahimović, was clinical and ruthless. Ibrahimović, who had joined Inter from Juventus in 2006, quickly became the focal point of the team's offense, using his unique blend of skill, strength, and flair to torment defenders and score crucial goals.

The 2007-2008 season saw Inter Milan continue their dominance in Serie A. Roberto Mancini's side retained the Scudetto, finishing the season with 85 points, three points ahead of Roma. Although the title race was more closely contested than the previous year, Inter's resilience and ability to win crucial matches ensured that they remained at the top of Italian football. The club's success was also a testament to Mancini's tactical acumen and his ability to manage a squad full of stars and egos, keeping them focused on the common goal of winning trophies.

However, despite their domestic success, Inter Milan faced challenges in Europe. The club's performances in the UEFA Champions League were inconsistent, with early exits in the knockout stages becoming a recurring theme. The inability to translate their domestic dominance into European success was a source of frustration for Moratti and the supporters, who longed for the club to reclaim its place among the elite in European football. This gap between domestic and European performances set the stage for one of the most significant managerial appointments in the club's history.

José Mourinho's Arrival (2008)

In the summer of 2008, Inter Milan made a bold and decisive move by appointing José Mourinho as head coach. Mourinho, already a household name in world football, had built a reputation as one of the most successful and charismatic managers of his generation. His achievements included winning the UEFA Champions League with Porto in 2004 and leading Chelsea to back-to-back Premier League titles. Known for his tactical brilliance, psychological acumen, and ability to build winning teams, Mourinho was seen as the ideal candidate to take Inter Milan to the next level.

Mourinho's arrival at Inter Milan was met with great anticipation and excitement. The club's hierarchy, led by Moratti, believed that Mourinho had the pedigree and experience to deliver the European success that had eluded them for so long. Mourinho himself was eager to prove his worth in Italian football, a league known for its tactical sophistication and defensive solidity. His task was clear: to continue Inter's domestic dominance while making a serious push for the UEFA Champions League.

Mourinho's impact at Inter Milan was immediate. Known for his meticulous preparation and attention to detail, Mourinho quickly set about instilling his philosophy in the team. His approach was characterized by a strong emphasis on defensive organization, tactical flexibility, and mental toughness. Mourinho's teams were known for their ability to adapt to different opponents and situations, and he brought this adaptability to Inter, making them a more versatile and resilient side.

One of Mourinho's key achievements in his first season (2008-2009) was to secure Inter's fourth consecutive Serie A title. The team finished the season with 84 points, 10 points clear of second-placed Juventus. Ibrahimović was once again the star of the show, finishing as the league's top scorer with 25 goals. Mourinho's ability to get the best out of his players, particularly in crucial matches, was evident as Inter consistently delivered strong performances when it mattered most.

Mourinho's first season at Inter was also marked by his high-profile clashes with the Italian media and rival managers. Known for his outspoken personality and mind games, Mourinho did not shy away from controversy, often using his press conferences to deflect pressure from his players and put the spotlight on himself. His confrontational style endeared him to the Inter fans, who appreciated his passion and commitment to the club, but it also made him a polarizing figure in Italian football.

Despite the domestic success, Mourinho's first season at Inter was marred by another disappointing exit in the Champions League. Inter were eliminated in the Round of 16 by Manchester United, highlighting the gap that still existed between the club and Europe's elite. Mourinho recognized that further reinforcements were needed to compete at the highest level, and he convinced Moratti to invest in new players for the following season.

The 2010 Treble: A Historic Achievement

The 2009-2010 season would go down as the most successful in the history of Inter Milan, as the club achieved an unprecedented treble, winning the Serie A title, the Coppa Italia, and the UEFA Champions League. This historic achievement was the culmination of years of investment, ambition, and determination, and it solidified José Mourinho's legacy as one of the greatest managers in the history of the club.

Mourinho's preparation for the 2009-2010 season began with several key signings that would prove instrumental to the team's success. The departure of Zlatan Ibrahimović to Barcelona in a blockbuster transfer deal was offset by the arrival of several top-quality players, including Samuel Eto'o, Diego Milito, Thiago Motta, and Wesley Sneijder. Each of these players would play a crucial role in Inter's treble-winning campaign.

The Serie A campaign was fiercely contested, with Inter facing stiff competition from Roma and AC Milan. However, Mourinho's tactical acumen and the team's resilience saw them through, as Inter secured the Scudetto on the final day of the season. The title win was Inter's fifth consecutive Serie A championship, a remarkable achievement that underscored the club's domestic dominance under Mourinho's leadership.

In the Coppa Italia, Inter faced Roma in the final, a match that was seen as a test of the team's mental strength ahead of the Champions League final. Inter emerged victorious with a 1-0 win, thanks to a goal from Milito, who had become one of the most reliable and clinical forwards in Europe. The victory in the Coppa Italia was a significant achievement in its own right, but it also served as a prelude to the most important match of the season: the UEFA Champions League final.

Inter's journey to the Champions League final was marked by a series of memorable performances. After navigating the group stage and the Round of 16, Inter faced Chelsea in the quarter-finals, with Mourinho coming up against his former club. Inter won both legs, advancing to the semi-finals, where they faced the mighty Barcelona, the reigning champions and widely regarded as the best team in the world at the time.

The semi-final against Barcelona was a tactical masterclass from Mourinho. In the first leg at the San Siro, Inter secured a 3-1 victory, with goals from Sneijder, Maicon, and Milito. The second leg at the Camp Nou was a defensive masterclass, as Inter, reduced to 10 men after the early dismissal of Motta, held on to a 1-0 defeat, winning 3-2 on aggregate to advance to the final. The victory over Barcelona was seen as a defining moment in Mourinho's career, as he outmaneuvered Pep Guardiola's side with a display of tactical discipline and mental fortitude.

The UEFA Champions League final, held on May 22, 2010, at the Santiago Bernabéu Stadium in Madrid, pitted Inter Milan against Bayern Munich. The match was a fitting climax to Inter's season, and Mourinho's tactical approach once again proved decisive. Diego Milito, who had been in sensational form throughout the campaign, scored both goals in a 2-0 victory, securing Inter's first European Cup since 1965. Milito's performances throughout the season earned him the nickname "Il Principe" (The Prince), and he was widely regarded as one of the best strikers in the world.

The 2010 Champions League victory completed Inter Milan's historic treble, making them the first Italian club to achieve this feat. The treble was a testament to the quality, depth, and resilience of the squad, as well as Mourinho's ability to build a team capable of winning on multiple fronts. The celebrations that followed were unforgettable, with fans flooding the streets of Milan to celebrate the club's greatest achievement.

For Massimo Moratti, the treble was the realization of a dream that he had pursued since taking over the club in 1995. The success vindicated his investments and his unwavering commitment to the club, and it solidified his legacy as one of the most important figures in the history of Inter Milan. The treble also cemented José Mourinho's place as one of the greatest managers in the history of football. His tactical brilliance, leadership, and ability to motivate his players to perform at their best on the biggest stages were key factors in Inter's historic achievement.

The 2010 treble marked the pinnacle of Inter Milan's modern era, a period of unprecedented success that was built on the foundations laid by Moratti's vision, the club's investment in top talent, and the tactical genius of José Mourinho. The treble-winning season remains the most celebrated chapter in the history of Inter Milan, a reminder of what the club is capable of when all the pieces come together.

The legacy of the 2010 treble continues to resonate with Inter Milan and its supporters. The achievements of that season set a standard for future generations, serving as both an inspiration and a benchmark for the club's ongoing pursuit of excellence. The memories of that historic campaign are etched into the fabric of the club, a symbol of what can be achieved through ambition, determination, and unity.

Chapter 18: Post-Mourinho Challenges

The Immediate Post-Mourinho Era (2010-2012)

The departure of José Mourinho from Inter Milan in the summer of 2010, shortly after leading the club to an historic treble, marked the end of one of the most successful periods in the club's history. Mourinho's decision to leave for Real Madrid left a void that would prove difficult to fill, and the immediate post-Mourinho era was characterized by a series of challenges as the club struggled to maintain the momentum of their recent successes.

Mourinho's departure came at a time when Inter Milan was at the pinnacle of European football. The club had just secured the Serie A title, the Coppa Italia, and the UEFA Champions League, and expectations were high for the future. However, the loss of Mourinho, a manager known for his tactical brilliance, leadership, and ability to get the best out of his players, was a significant blow. The task of finding a suitable successor to maintain the level of success achieved under Mourinho was daunting.

To replace Mourinho, Inter Milan appointed Rafael Benítez, a Spanish manager with a proven track record, including winning the UEFA Champions League with Liverpool in 2005. Benítez was seen as a manager who could bring stability and continue the club's winning ways. However, the transition from Mourinho to Benítez was far from smooth. The squad, still basking in the glory of the treble, found it difficult to adjust to Benítez's methods and philosophy. The Spanish coach's more reserved and methodical approach contrasted sharply with Mourinho's intense and charismatic style, leading to tension within the squad.

The 2010-2011 season began with Inter Milan winning the Supercoppa Italiana, defeating Roma 3-1, but it quickly became apparent that all was not well. Inter's performances in Serie A were inconsistent, and the team struggled to replicate the dominance they had shown under Mourinho. Injuries to key players, including Diego Milito and Wesley Sneijder, further complicated matters, as the squad depth was tested. In the Champions League, Inter managed to advance from the group stage, but their performances lacked the intensity and precision that had defined their play in the previous season.

The situation came to a head in December 2010, when Benítez publicly criticized the club's management for not providing sufficient support in the transfer market. His comments, coupled with the team's poor form in Serie A, where they found themselves well off the pace in the title race, led to his dismissal just six months into his tenure. Benítez's short-lived spell at Inter was emblematic of the challenges the club faced in the immediate aftermath of Mourinho's departure—an inability to find the right balance and cohesion under new leadership.

In an attempt to steady the ship, Inter Milan appointed Leonardo, a former AC Milan player and manager, as Benítez's replacement. Leonardo's arrival brought a temporary boost in morale and performance. Under his guidance, Inter climbed back up the Serie A table, eventually finishing second behind AC Milan. Leonardo also led Inter to victory in the Coppa Italia, defeating Palermo 3-1 in the final. However, despite these successes, the team's vulnerabilities were exposed in the Champions League, where they were eliminated by Schalke 04 in the quarter-finals, suffering a humiliating 7-3 aggregate defeat.

Leonardo's tenure, while more successful than Benítez's, was also short-lived. At the end of the 2010-2011 season, Leonardo left Inter Milan to take up a role as sporting director at Paris Saint-Germain, leaving the club once again searching for a new manager. The constant changes in the dugout, coupled with the aging of key players from the treble-winning squad, made it increasingly difficult for Inter to maintain their status as one of Europe's elite clubs.

The 2011-2012 season saw Inter Milan appoint Gian Piero Gasperini as head coach. Gasperini, known for his innovative 3-4-3 formation, was expected to bring a fresh approach to the team. However, his tenure quickly turned into a disaster. The squad struggled to adapt to his tactics, and a string of poor results, including a shock defeat to newly promoted Novara, led to his dismissal after just five games in charge.

Claudio Ranieri was brought in as Gasperini's replacement, and while he managed to stabilize the team somewhat, the results were still far from what was expected of a club of Inter's stature. The team finished sixth in Serie A, missing out on Champions League qualification for the first time since 2003. The struggles of the 2011-2012 season highlighted the difficulties Inter faced in the post-Mourinho era—a lack of stability in management, an aging squad, and an inability to consistently compete at the highest level.

Struggles for Stability (2012-2015)

The period from 2012 to 2015 was marked by continued struggles for stability at Inter Milan. The club, once a dominant force in Italian and European football, found itself in a prolonged period of transition, characterized by frequent changes in management, inconsistent performances, and a search for a new identity.

The 2012-2013 season began with the appointment of Andrea Stramaccioni as head coach. Stramaccioni, who had impressed as the coach of Inter's youth team, was given the opportunity to lead the senior squad on a permanent basis after a brief interim stint at the end of the previous season. His appointment was seen as a bold move, as he was relatively inexperienced at the top level. Despite a promising start to the season, which included a memorable 3-1 victory over Juventus in Turin, the team's form quickly deteriorated. Injuries to key players, including Diego Milito, and a lack of squad depth contributed to Inter's struggles. The team finished a disappointing ninth in Serie A, their lowest finish in over a decade.

Stramaccioni's tenure was marked by inconsistency and an inability to find a tactical system that suited the squad. The lack of continuity in management, combined with the aging core of the team, made it difficult for Inter to compete with the top clubs in Serie A. The absence of European football further compounded the club's struggles, as the financial impact of missing out on the Champions League began to take its toll.

In May 2013, Stramaccioni was dismissed, and Inter Milan appointed Walter Mazzarri as his successor. Mazzarri, who had enjoyed success at Napoli, was seen as a more experienced and pragmatic manager who could bring stability to the club. His appointment marked a shift towards a more conservative and defensively solid approach, as Mazzarri implemented his preferred 3-5-2 formation. The 2013-2014 season saw some improvement, with Inter finishing fifth in Serie A and qualifying for the Europa League. However, the team's performances were still well below the standards expected of a club of Inter's stature.

Mazzarri's tenure was characterized by a focus on defensive organization and counter-attacking football, but his conservative approach was often criticized for lacking creativity and flair. The team struggled to break down weaker opponents, and while they were defensively solid, they lacked the attacking firepower needed to challenge for the top spots in Serie A. Mazzarri's pragmatic style, while effective to a degree, did not align with the expectations of the fans or the club's management.

The 2014-2015 season began with renewed optimism, but it quickly became clear that

Mazzarri's approach was not producing the desired results. After a series of poor performances, including a disappointing start to the Europa League campaign, Mazzarri was dismissed in November 2014. His departure marked yet another managerial change, as Inter Milan continued to search for the right formula to return to the top.

In a surprising move, Inter Milan reappointed Roberto Mancini as head coach in November 2014. Mancini, who had previously led Inter to three consecutive Serie A titles between 2005 and 2008, was seen as a familiar and trusted figure who could restore the club's fortunes. His return brought a renewed sense of hope, as he sought to rebuild the squad and instill a winning mentality.

Mancini's second stint at Inter Milan was marked by a focus on rebuilding the team and laying the foundations for future success. He made several key signings, including bringing in players like Xherdan Shaqiri and Lukas Podolski, in an attempt to add creativity and firepower to the squad. However, the results were mixed, as the team continued to struggle with consistency. Inter finished eighth in Serie A, once again missing out on European qualification.

The period from 2012 to 2015 was a challenging time for Inter Milan, as the club grappled with the difficulties of rebuilding in the post-Mourinho era. The frequent changes in management, coupled with an aging squad and a lack of continuity, made it difficult for the club to find stability. The financial pressures of missing out on Champions League football also limited the club's ability to invest in top talent, further complicating the rebuilding process.

Despite these challenges, there were signs of progress, particularly with the return of Roberto Mancini, who brought a sense of direction and purpose to the club. The focus on rebuilding the squad and developing a more cohesive playing style laid the groundwork for future improvements. However, the struggles for stability during this period highlighted the challenges faced by Inter Milan as they sought to navigate the complexities of modern football and return to the heights they had reached during the Mourinho era.

Chapter 19: The Zhang Era

The Acquisition by Suning Holdings (2016)

The summer of 2016 marked a significant turning point in the history of Inter Milan with the acquisition of the club by Suning Holdings Group, a Chinese retail giant. The deal, valued at around €270 million, saw Suning acquire a 70% majority stake in Inter Milan, with the remaining shares held by the previous owners, including the club's president Erick Thohir, and Massimo Moratti, who maintained a symbolic minority stake. This acquisition ushered in a new era for Inter Milan, one characterized by increased financial investment, modernization, and a renewed ambition to return to the top of Italian and European football.

Suning Holdings, led by chairman Zhang Jindong, was one of China's largest privately-owned companies, with interests ranging from retail to media and sports. Their entry into the world of European football through the acquisition of Inter Milan was part of a broader strategy to expand their global footprint and leverage the club's brand to further their business interests. The acquisition was also aligned with China's growing interest in football, spurred by the government's push to develop the sport domestically and enhance the country's influence on the global stage.

The immediate impact of the Suning acquisition was felt in the club's financial situation. Under Suning's ownership, Inter Milan gained access to significant financial resources, allowing the club to invest in new players, improve infrastructure, and enhance its commercial operations. The acquisition marked the beginning of a period of financial stability and growth for the club, which had struggled with debt and limited spending power in the years leading up to the takeover.

One of the key figures in this new era was Steven Zhang, the son of Zhang Jindong. In October 2018, Steven Zhang was appointed as the president of Inter Milan, making him the youngest president in the club's history at just 26 years old. Zhang's appointment was a clear signal of Suning's commitment to the club and its long-term vision for success. Despite his youth, Zhang quickly established himself as a dynamic and forward-thinking leader, dedicated to restoring Inter Milan's glory days while also modernizing the club for the challenges of the 21st century.

Under Steven Zhang's leadership, Inter Milan embarked on a process of modernization and restructuring. The club focused on enhancing its global brand, expanding its commercial partnerships, and leveraging digital platforms to engage with fans around the world. Zhang's approach was marked by a blend of traditional values and innovative thinking, as he sought to honor the club's rich history while positioning it as a modern, global powerhouse.

One of Zhang's early moves was to invest in the squad, bringing in high-profile players to strengthen the team. In the summer of 2016, Inter signed João Mário from Sporting CP, Antonio Candreva from Lazio, and Gabriel Barbosa from Santos, signaling the club's intent to compete at the highest level. However, despite these signings, the team struggled to find consistency in Serie A, and the 2016-2017 season ended with a disappointing seventh-place finish.

Recognizing the need for strong leadership on the pitch, Zhang and Suning turned their attention to the managerial position. In June 2017, Luciano Spalletti was appointed as head coach, bringing with him a wealth of experience from his successful spells at Roma and Zenit Saint Petersburg. Spalletti's appointment marked the beginning of a more stable period for Inter Milan, as he implemented a tactical system that emphasized defensive organization and quick transitions. Under his guidance, Inter Milan qualified for the UEFA Champions League in the

2017-2018 season, finishing fourth in Serie A—a significant improvement from previous years.

Steven Zhang's leadership during this period was characterized by a clear vision and a willingness to make bold decisions. He was instrumental in securing key sponsorship deals and partnerships that boosted the club's revenue and global profile. Zhang also emphasized the importance of the club's youth academy, investing in the development of young talent as part of a long-term strategy to build a sustainable and competitive team.

Despite these positive developments, the path to restoring Inter Milan's dominance in Serie A remained challenging. The competition in the league was fierce, with Juventus continuing to dominate domestically. However, Zhang and Suning remained committed to their vision, determined to bring the Scudetto back to the blue and black side of Milan.

The Road to the 2021 Scudetto (2016-2021)

The journey towards Inter Milan's 2021 Serie A title was a culmination of years of investment, strategic planning, and determination under the leadership of Steven Zhang and the management of Antonio Conte. This period was marked by a gradual but steady progression, as Inter Milan worked to close the gap on their rivals and eventually reclaim their place at the top of Italian football.

Antonio Conte's arrival at Inter Milan in the summer of 2019 was a pivotal moment in the club's resurgence. Conte, a proven winner with a track record of success at Juventus and Chelsea, was brought in to instill a winning mentality and take the team to the next level. His appointment was a clear statement of intent from Steven Zhang and Suning Holdings, who were determined to end Juventus' nine-year dominance of Serie A and bring the Scudetto back to Inter.

Conte's impact was immediate. Known for his intense work ethic, tactical acumen, and ability to get the best out of his players, Conte quickly set about transforming Inter Milan into a cohesive, disciplined, and competitive unit. He implemented his preferred 3-5-2 formation, which emphasized defensive solidity, wing-back play, and quick transitions from defense to attack. Conte's system required a high level of fitness, tactical intelligence, and commitment from the players, and he worked tirelessly to instill these qualities in the squad.

The summer of 2019 saw significant investment in the squad, with several key signings that would play crucial roles in Inter's eventual success. Romelu Lukaku was brought in from Manchester United for a club-record fee, and his arrival proved to be a masterstroke. Lukaku quickly became the focal point of Inter's attack, forming a lethal partnership with Lautaro Martínez. His strength, pace, and clinical finishing made him one of the most feared strikers in Serie A, and his leadership on and off the pitch was invaluable.

Other notable signings included Diego Godín, a veteran center-back with a wealth of experience, and Nicolò Barella, a dynamic midfielder with great potential. These additions, along with the existing core of players like Samir Handanović, Milan Škriniar, and Marcelo Brozović, gave Conte the tools he needed to build a team capable of challenging for the title.

The 2019-2020 season saw Inter Milan make significant strides under Conte's leadership. The team finished second in Serie A, just one point behind Juventus, and reached the final of the UEFA Europa League, where they were narrowly defeated by Sevilla. While the season ended without silverware, it was clear that Inter Milan were on the right track. The progress made under Conte was evident, and the team's performances in both domestic and European competitions were a marked improvement from previous years.

The 2020-2021 season was the culmination of Inter Milan's journey towards the Scudetto. With the foundation laid in the previous season, Conte and his team entered the campaign with renewed focus and determination. The season was challenging, with the COVID-19 pandemic continuing to impact football across the globe, but Inter Milan rose to the occasion. Conte's tactical approach, built around a solid defense and a potent attack, proved to be the perfect formula for success.

Romelu Lukaku and Lautaro Martínez, known as "LuLa," were instrumental in Inter's title charge. The duo combined for over 40 goals in the league, with Lukaku finishing as the team's top scorer. Lukaku's ability to hold up the ball, bring others into play, and score crucial goals made him the standout player of the season. Martínez's movement, work rate, and finishing complemented Lukaku perfectly, and together they formed one of the most effective strike partnerships in Europe.

In midfield, Nicolò Barella emerged as one of Serie A's best players, combining energy, creativity, and tenacity. His performances were key to Inter's success, as he provided the link between defense and attack. Marcelo Brozović, playing in a deep-lying playmaker role, dictated the tempo of the game, while Arturo Vidal and Christian Eriksen added experience and quality to the midfield.

Defensively, Inter Milan were rock solid. The back three of Milan Škriniar, Stefan de Vrij, and Alessandro Bastoni, protected by the ever-reliable Samir Handanović in goal, formed the best defense in the league. Conte's emphasis on defensive organization and discipline paid off, as Inter conceded the fewest goals in Serie A. The wing-backs, Achraf Hakimi and Ashley Young, provided width and pace, contributing both defensively and offensively.

Inter Milan's consistency throughout the season was remarkable. The team went on a 19-match unbeaten run in the league, including crucial victories over Juventus, AC Milan, and Lazio. Conte's ability to motivate his players and maintain their focus in the face of pressure was a key factor in their success. The team's resilience, mental toughness, and tactical discipline were evident in every match, as they ground out results and maintained their lead at the top of the table.

On May 2, 2021, Inter Milan were crowned Serie A champions, securing their first Scudetto in 11 years and ending Juventus' nine-year reign as champions. The title win was a moment of immense joy and pride for the club, its supporters, and the leadership under Steven Zhang. The Scudetto was a testament to the hard work, dedication, and vision of everyone involved in the club, from the players and coaching staff to the management and ownership.

For Steven Zhang, the 2021 Scudetto was the fulfillment of a promise he had made when he became president in 2018. It marked the culmination of a five-year journey under Suning Holdings, during which the club had undergone significant transformation both on and off the pitch. Zhang's leadership, characterized by a blend of ambition, innovation, and respect for the club's traditions, played a crucial role in Inter's revival.

The 2021 Scudetto was not just a return to the top of Italian football; it was a statement of intent from Inter Milan. The club's journey from the acquisition by Suning Holdings in 2016 to the title win in 2021 was a testament to the power of vision, investment, and strong leadership. The Zhang era, marked by the acquisition, Steven Zhang's presidency, and Antonio Conte's management, had brought Inter Milan back to the pinnacle of Serie A, restoring the club's status as one of the giants of Italian football.

The success of the Zhang era has laid a strong foundation for the future, as Inter Milan looks to build on their Scudetto win and compete at the highest level in Europe. The journey to the 2021

Scudetto was a story of resilience, determination, and the realization of a long-held dream—a story that will be remembered as one of the defining chapters in the history of Inter Milan.

Chapter 20: Inter Milan in the 2020s

Inter Milan's Performance in European Competitions (2020-Present)

The 2020s have been a transformative decade for Inter Milan, marked by a return to prominence in both domestic and European competitions. After a challenging period in the mid-2010s, Inter Milan began to re-establish themselves as a force in European football, particularly under the leadership of coaches like Antonio Conte and Simone Inzaghi.

During the early part of the decade, Inter Milan made significant strides in the UEFA Champions League. In the 2022-2023 season, under Simone Inzaghi, the team reached the final of the competition for the first time since their historic treble-winning season in 2010. This was a remarkable achievement, given the challenges posed by the strength of their European rivals. Inter's journey to the final was characterized by tactical discipline, solid defensive performances, and effective counter-attacking play, which became hallmarks of Inzaghi's management style. Although Inter narrowly lost to Manchester City in the final, their performances throughout the tournament solidified their reputation as one of Europe's elite clubs once again.

Key players during this period included Lautaro Martínez, who continued to develop as one of the best forwards in Europe, and Nicolò Barella, whose dynamic midfield presence was crucial in both domestic and European competitions. Defensively, the leadership of players like Milan Škriniar and Alessandro Bastoni provided the foundation for Inter's success in high-pressure matches. Additionally, the tactical acumen of Simone Inzaghi, particularly his ability to adapt the team's formation and approach based on the opposition, played a crucial role in their deep runs in European competitions.

Winning the 2024 Scudetto and Obtaining the Second Star

The pinnacle of Inter Milan's recent achievements came with their victory in the 2023-2024 Serie A season, where they secured their 20th Scudetto. This triumph was not only significant for ending a brief title drought but also for what it symbolized—Inter Milan's resurgence to the top of Italian football. The 20th league title meant that Inter earned the right to add a second star to their iconic black and blue jersey, a prestigious symbol that marked their two-decade dominance in Italian football.

The 2023-2024 season was a testament to the resilience and tactical brilliance of the team, once again managed by Simone Inzaghi. Despite facing financial challenges and the necessity to sell key players in previous seasons, Inzaghi managed to build a squad capable of dethroning Juventus and AC Milan, who had been strong contenders throughout the season. Inter's defensive solidity, combined with a potent attack led by Martínez and supported by players like Federico Dimarco and Denzel Dumfries, proved to be the winning formula. The decisive moment of the season came when Inter secured the Scudetto with a victory over their city rivals AC Milan in the Derby della Madonnina, a result that also ensured their superiority in the Milanese head-to-head record.

Future Aspirations and Challenges

Looking ahead, Inter Milan faces a mix of opportunities and challenges as they seek to build on their recent successes. Financial stability remains a concern, with the club needing to manage significant debt levels while maintaining competitiveness on the pitch. The involvement of Suning Holdings and the leadership of Steven Zhang have provided crucial support, but the economic realities of modern football, including the implications of the COVID-19 pandemic and global market fluctuations, continue to pose risks.

Strategically, Inter's future will likely involve balancing the need for immediate success with sustainable growth. This could mean a continued focus on developing young talent from their academy, shrewd investments in the transfer market, and maintaining strong partnerships with commercial sponsors. Ensuring the retention of key figures like Simone Inzaghi, who has proven capable of navigating the complexities of Serie A and European football, will be crucial for the club's ongoing success.

Moreover, Inter Milan's ambitions extend beyond domestic dominance. The club aims to once again challenge for the UEFA Champions League, a trophy that has eluded them since 2010. The foundation laid in recent seasons, combined with the tactical experience gained from deep runs in the competition, positions Inter as a formidable contender in the coming years.

As Inter Milan moves forward into the latter half of the 2020s, the club's leadership, under the stewardship of Steven Zhang, will need to navigate these challenges while keeping an eye on the ultimate goal—restoring Inter Milan to the pinnacle of European football and ensuring their legacy continues to grow.

Chapter 21: The Legacy of Inter Milan

Inter Milan's Contribution to Italian Football

Inter Milan's legacy in Italian football is profound, having played a pivotal role in shaping both the tactical evolution and cultural identity of the sport in Italy. From the club's early days to its modern triumphs, Inter has been at the forefront of innovation and excellence in football.

One of the most significant contributions Inter Milan made to Italian football was the introduction and popularization of the *Catenaccio* system under Helenio Herrera in the 1960s. *Catenaccio*, which translates to "door-bolt," emphasized a strong defensive structure, with a sweeper (or *libero*) behind the backline to clean up any loose balls. This tactical system was revolutionary at the time and became synonymous with Italian football's reputation for defensive solidity. Under Herrera's guidance, Inter Milan mastered this approach, leading them to two consecutive European Cup victories in 1964 and 1965, along with multiple Serie A titles. The success of *Catenaccio* not only brought Inter international acclaim but also influenced generations of Italian coaches and teams, who adapted and evolved the system into various defensive strategies that are still seen today.

In addition to tactical innovation, Inter Milan has been a pioneer in embracing multiculturalism and diversity within the sport. The club's nickname, *Nerazzurri* (The Black and Blues), also symbolizes the club's openness to players from all backgrounds. Inter has a long history of integrating international talent, reflecting Milan's cosmopolitan identity. This multicultural approach helped the club build a strong team dynamic and introduced Italian fans to a wide range of playing styles and cultures. Players like Jair da Costa, Ronaldo, Javier Zanetti, and Samuel Eto'o not only brought their individual brilliance to the team but also enriched the tactical and cultural fabric of Italian football.

Inter Milan's influence extends beyond the pitch. The club has been a symbol of resilience and pride in the city of Milan, particularly during times of social and economic challenges. The rivalry with AC Milan, known as the *Derby della Madonnina*, is one of the most storied and passionate in world football. It reflects not just a footballing contest but also a cultural clash between different social and political identities within the city. Inter's victories in these derbies have often been seen as triumphs of certain values and ideologies, further embedding the club in the cultural psyche of Milan and Italy as a whole.

The Global Reach of Inter Milan

Inter Milan's legacy is not confined to Italy; the club has established itself as a global brand with a significant international following. Over the decades, Inter has cultivated a passionate fanbase that spans continents, reflecting the club's success on the pitch and its efforts to engage with supporters around the world.

The globalization of football in the late 20th and early 21st centuries allowed Inter Milan to expand its reach far beyond Italy. The club's success in European competitions, particularly during the 1960s and again in the 2010s, played a crucial role in boosting its international profile. The treble-winning season of 2009-2010, under José Mourinho, was a defining moment that cemented Inter's status as a global powerhouse. The victory in the UEFA Champions League final against Bayern Munich not only brought joy to millions of Inter fans but also attracted new supporters from around the world who were captivated by the team's style of play and resilience.

Inter Milan has also made significant strides in enhancing its global brand through strategic partnerships, digital engagement, and international tours. The acquisition of the club by Suning Holdings in 2016 marked a new era of globalization for Inter.

Suning's extensive business network in Asia, particularly in China, provided the club with a platform to connect with millions of new fans in one of the world's largest and most rapidly growing football markets. Under the leadership of Steven Zhang, Inter has invested heavily in digital content, social media engagement, and global marketing campaigns, further expanding its reach and solidifying its brand internationally.

The club's global reach is also evident in its diverse fanbase, which includes supporters from Europe, Asia, the Americas, and Africa. Inter Milan's official fan clubs, known as *Inter Club*, are spread across the globe, fostering a sense of community among fans regardless of geographical location. These fan clubs play a vital role in maintaining the club's global presence, organizing events, watch parties, and charity initiatives that bring fans together and strengthen their connection to the club.

Moreover, Inter's involvement in charitable activities and social initiatives has further enhanced its global reputation. The club has been active in promoting social causes, including initiatives focused on education, health, and inclusion. Through partnerships with international organizations and foundations, Inter Milan has used its platform to make a positive impact on communities around the world, reinforcing the idea that football can be a force for good beyond the confines of the pitch.

San Siro: Inter Milan's Iconic Home

San Siro, officially known as Stadio Giuseppe Meazza, is not just the home of Inter Milan; it is one of the most iconic stadiums in world football. Located in the heart of Milan, San Siro has been the stage for some of the most memorable moments in football history and is deeply intertwined with the identity and legacy of Inter Milan.

Opened in 1926, San Siro was initially built to serve as the home ground for AC Milan. However, in 1947, Inter Milan moved into the stadium, and since then, the two Milanese giants have shared it, making San Siro one of the few stadiums in the world to host two major football clubs. The stadium was renamed Stadio Giuseppe Meazza in 1980, in honor of the legendary Italian footballer who played for both Milan clubs but is more closely associated with Inter Milan, where he achieved great success.

San Siro has a seating capacity of over 75,000, making it one of the largest stadiums in Europe. Its distinctive architecture, characterized by its towering spiral ramps and massive concrete structure, has made it a symbol of Milan's footballing heritage. Over the decades, San Siro has hosted numerous high-profile matches, including World Cup games, European Championship finals, and UEFA Champions League finals. For Inter Milan fans, the stadium is a fortress, a place where the club's history and identity are celebrated, and where unforgettable memories have been made.

One of the most significant aspects of San Siro is its role in the *Derby della Madonnina*. The atmosphere during these derby matches is electric, with the stadium split between the passionate supporters of Inter and AC Milan. The choreography, chants, and intense rivalry create a unique experience that is renowned worldwide. For Inter Milan, San Siro has been the backdrop for some of the club's greatest victories over their city rivals, adding to the stadium's legendary status.

As Inter Milan looks to the future, the question of San Siro's fate has become a topic of intense discussion. Both Inter Milan and AC Milan have expressed interest in building a new, state-of-the-art stadium to replace San Siro, reflecting the need for modern facilities that can generate greater revenue and provide a better experience for fans. The proposed new stadium, tentatively named the "Cathedral," is expected to be a modern architectural marvel that will serve as a symbol of Milan's future while paying homage to its rich footballing past.

The potential move from San Siro represents a significant moment in Inter Milan's history. While the new stadium promises to bring numerous benefits, the decision to leave behind such an iconic venue is not taken lightly. For many fans, San Siro is more than just a stadium; it is a sacred place where generations of supporters have come together to celebrate their love for Inter Milan. The future of San Siro, whether it will be preserved in some capacity or replaced entirely, remains uncertain, but its legacy as one of the most storied stadiums in football history is secure.

San Siro's importance to Inter Milan's identity cannot be overstated. It has been the setting for the club's greatest triumphs and most heartbreaking defeats, and it holds a special place in the hearts of Inter fans. As the club moves forward, the memories of San Siro will continue to inspire future generations, serving as a reminder of the rich history and tradition that have made Inter Milan one of the most respected and successful clubs in the world.

Chapter 22: Inter Milan's Greatest Moments

Memorable Derbies and Rivalries

Inter Milan's history is deeply intertwined with its rivalries, most notably the *Derby della Madonnina* against AC Milan, but also other significant rivalries that have defined Italian football. These matches are more than just games; they are cultural events that capture the passion, pride, and identity of the club and its supporters.

The *Derby della Madonnina* is undoubtedly the most significant fixture in Inter Milan's calendar. Named after the statue of the Virgin Mary that sits atop Milan's cathedral, this derby is one of the most storied rivalries in world football. It divides the city of Milan into blue and black (Inter) and red and black (AC Milan), with families, friends, and workplaces often split by allegiance. The rivalry began in earnest in 1908 when Inter was formed as a breakaway club from AC Milan, and it has only intensified over the decades.

One of the most memorable derbies in recent history was the 6-0 victory for AC Milan on May 11, 2001. This humiliating defeat for Inter remains one of the darkest days in the club's history. However, Inter responded emphatically a few years later on October 29, 2006, with a 4-3 victory, which is considered one of the greatest derbies in history. In that match, Inter raced to a 4-1 lead before AC Milan mounted a late comeback, but Inter held on for a dramatic win. The victory was a turning point, symbolizing Inter's resurgence and eventual dominance in Serie A under Roberto Mancini and later José Mourinho.

Another unforgettable derby took place on March 28, 2004, when Inter won 3-2 in a thrilling encounter. Adriano scored the winning goal in the 85th minute, sending the Inter faithful into raptures. This match was significant not only because of the victory but also because it marked the beginning of Inter's growing dominance over their city rivals in the mid-2000s.

Beyond the *Derby della Madonnina*, Inter Milan has fierce rivalries with Juventus and AS Roma. The rivalry with Juventus, known as the *Derby d'Italia*, is particularly intense. This fixture pits the two most successful clubs in Italian football against each other, with matches often carrying significant implications for the Serie A title. The rivalry was further inflamed by the Calciopoli scandal in 2006, which saw Juventus stripped of titles and Inter awarded the 2005-2006 Scudetto. The matches that followed were charged with emotion, as both clubs sought to assert their dominance in Italian football.

One of the most significant encounters in this rivalry was the 2018-2019 season's 1-1 draw at the San Siro, where Inter's defensive resilience showcased their ability to compete with the best.

The rivalry with AS Roma also deserves mention, particularly due to the intense battles for the Coppa Italia and Supercoppa Italiana during the 2000s. Inter and Roma faced each other in the Coppa Italia final for four consecutive years from 2005 to 2008, with each encounter adding to the growing animosity between the two clubs. These matches were often characterized by their high stakes, physical intensity, and moments of individual brilliance.

Greatest Matches in Inter Milan's History

Inter Milan's history is replete with iconic matches that have defined the club's legacy. From thrilling domestic encounters to epic European nights, these games have left an indelible mark on the hearts of Inter fans and the annals of football history.

One of the greatest matches in Inter Milan's history was the second leg of the 1964 European Cup final against Real Madrid, played at the Prater Stadium in Vienna. Inter, under the guidance of Helenio Herrera, secured their first European Cup with a 3-1 victory. Sandro Mazzola scored twice, and Aurelio

Milani added another to secure the triumph against a Real Madrid side that had dominated European football in the late 1950s and early 1960s. This victory was not only a significant achievement for Inter but also a watershed moment for Italian football, as it established Serie A as a force in European competition.

Another unforgettable match came in the 2010 UEFA Champions League semi-final against Barcelona. Inter, managed by José Mourinho, faced the reigning European champions in what was billed as a clash of titans. After securing a 3-1 victory in the first leg at the San Siro, Inter traveled to the Camp Nou for the return leg, knowing they faced a monumental task. Despite being reduced to 10 men after Thiago Motta's early red card, Inter produced one of the most resolute defensive performances in Champions League history. Although they lost 1-0 on the night, they advanced to the final on aggregate, where they would eventually claim the title by defeating Bayern Munich. The match against Barcelona is often cited as one of the greatest examples of tactical discipline and mental resilience in football history.

Domestically, Inter's 5-0 victory over Sampdoria on March 16, 1986, stands out as one of the club's most dominant performances. In this Serie A match, Inter completely outclassed their opponents, with Alessandro Altobelli scoring a hat-trick. The win was a showcase of Inter's attacking prowess during a period when they were beginning to establish themselves as serious title contenders.

Another significant match in Inter Milan's history was the 1998 UEFA Cup final against Lazio. Inter, led by coach Luigi Simoni, won 3-0 in a commanding performance, with goals from Iván Zamorano, Javier Zanetti, and Ronaldo. The victory was particularly sweet as it marked Ronaldo's first major European trophy and solidified his status as one of the greatest players in the world. The match also ended Inter's six-year wait for a major trophy, reigniting the club's ambitions for future success.

More recently, Inter's 3-2 victory over Juventus on September 18, 2016, stands out as one of the defining moments of the 2010s. Known as the "Derby d'Italia," this match saw Inter come from behind to defeat their arch-rivals, with goals from Mauro Icardi and Ivan Perišić. The win was crucial in boosting Inter's confidence and re-establishing their competitive edge against Juventus, who had dominated Italian football for the previous five years.

These matches, among many others, are woven into the fabric of Inter Milan's history. They are reminders of the club's capacity for greatness, the passion of its players and supporters, and the enduring legacy of a team that has consistently been at the forefront of Italian and European football. Each game has contributed to the rich tapestry of Inter Milan's story, a story that continues to inspire and captivate football fans around the world.

Chapter 23: The Legends of Inter Milan

Profiles of Iconic Players

Inter Milan's rich history is adorned with the contributions of legendary players who have left an indelible mark on the club and the world of football. These players, through their skill, leadership, and passion, have not only shaped the identity of Inter Milan but have also become icons of the sport.

Giuseppe Meazza (1927-1940, 1946-1947)

Giuseppe Meazza, after whom the San Siro stadium is co-named, is arguably the most iconic player in Inter Milan's history. A forward with incredible skill, vision, and goal-scoring ability, Meazza was instrumental in the club's early successes. He made his debut for Inter at the age of 17 and quickly became one of the most feared strikers in Europe. Meazza scored 284 goals in 408 appearances for Inter, making him the club's all-time top scorer. His influence extended beyond club football as he helped Italy win two World Cups in 1934 and 1938, further solidifying his legendary status. Meazza was known for his elegance on the ball and his ability to score from almost any position on the pitch. His legacy is so profound that he is still regarded as one of the greatest Italian footballers of all time.

Sandro Mazzola (1960-1977)

Sandro Mazzola is another legend who is synonymous with Inter Milan. The son of Valentino Mazzola, the captain of the Grande Torino team tragically lost in the Superga air disaster, Sandro carved out his own legacy at Inter. Mazzola was a key figure in Helenio Herrera's Grande Inter team of the 1960s. A versatile attacking midfielder, Mazzola was known for his dribbling, passing, and goal-scoring abilities. He played a crucial role in Inter's back-to-back European Cup victories in 1964 and 1965, as well as in their domestic successes. Mazzola's rivalry with Gianni Rivera of AC Milan was one of the highlights of Italian football in the 1960s, with the two often compared in debates over who was the better playmaker. Mazzola's loyalty to Inter was unwavering, and he remains one of the most beloved figures in the club's history.

Javier Zanetti (1995-2014)

Javier Zanetti, known as "Il Capitano," is one of the most respected and admired figures in the history of Inter Milan. Zanetti joined Inter in 1995 from Banfield and went on to become the most-capped player in the club's history, with 858 appearances over 19 seasons. A versatile player, Zanetti was capable of playing in multiple positions, including right-back, left-back, and midfield. He was renowned for his incredible stamina, leadership, and professionalism on and off the pitch. Zanetti captained Inter during one of the most successful periods in the club's history, leading the team to five Serie A titles, four Coppa Italia victories, and, most notably, the historic treble in 2010. Zanetti's commitment to Inter extended beyond his playing days, as he took on the role of vice-president of the club after his retirement, continuing to serve the team he loves.

Ronaldo (1997-2002)

Ronaldo Luís Nazário de Lima, simply known as Ronaldo, is one of the greatest players to have ever graced the football pitch, and his time at Inter Milan, although marred by injuries, is remembered with great affection. Ronaldo joined Inter in 1997 from Barcelona for a then-world record fee, and his impact was immediate. Known as "Il Fenomeno" (The Phenomenon), Ronaldo dazzled fans with his extraordinary dribbling, speed, and finishing. In his debut season, he scored 25 goals in Serie A and led Inter to the UEFA Cup title in 1998, where he scored a memorable goal in the final against Lazio. Despite suffering serious knee injuries that kept him out of action for extended periods, Ronaldo's talent and charisma made him a beloved figure at Inter. His ability to bounce back from adversity and his contribution to the club's successes during his time in Milan are part of what makes him a legend.

Giuseppe Bergomi (1979-1999)

Giuseppe Bergomi, often referred to as "Lo Zio" (The Uncle) due to his mature appearance from a young age, was a stalwart of Inter Milan's defense for two decades. Making his debut at just 16 years old, Bergomi went on to become one of the greatest defenders in Italian football history. Known for his tough tackling, intelligence, and leadership, Bergomi was a key figure in Inter's 1989 Scudetto-winning side and their success in European competitions, including the UEFA Cup triumphs in 1991, 1994, and 1998. His loyalty to Inter was unwavering, as he spent his entire career with the club, making over 750 appearances. Bergomi's consistency and dedication earned him the respect of teammates and opponents alike, and he remains a symbol of Inter's defensive resilience.

Managers Who Defined Inter Milan

Inter Milan's success over the years has been shaped not only by its legendary players but also by the managers who have brought tactical innovation, leadership, and vision to the club. These managers have left a lasting impact on Inter's history and have become synonymous with the club's greatest achievements.

Helenio Herrera (1960-1968, 1973-1974)

Helenio Herrera is perhaps the most influential manager in Inter Milan's history. Known as "Il Mago" (The Magician), Herrera revolutionized Italian football with his tactical innovations and psychological approach to management. He is most famous for popularizing the *Catenaccio* system at Inter, which focused on a strong defense and quick counter-attacks. Under Herrera's leadership, Inter Milan enjoyed its most successful period in the 1960s, winning three Serie A titles, two European Cups, and two Intercontinental Cups. Herrera was also a master motivator, using psychological techniques to instill confidence and discipline in his players. His influence on Inter Milan and Italian football as a whole is immeasurable, and his legacy as one of the greatest managers in football history is well-deserved.

Giovanni Trapattoni (1986-1991)

Giovanni Trapattoni brought a new level of professionalism and tactical discipline to Inter Milan when he took over as manager in 1986. Trapattoni, who had already enjoyed tremendous success with Juventus, implemented a robust and organized style of play that led Inter to the 1988-1989 Serie A title. That season, Inter set a then-record of 58 points in a 34-match season, showcasing their dominance. Trapattoni's Inter was known for its solid defense, led by players like Giuseppe Bergomi and Riccardo Ferri, and its efficient attack, featuring the likes of Aldo Serena and Lothar Matthäus. Trapattoni's success at Inter reinforced his reputation as one of the best managers in the world and further solidified his status as a tactical genius in Italian football.

José Mourinho (2008-2010)

José Mourinho's tenure at Inter Milan, though brief, was one of the most successful periods in the club's history. Known as "The Special One," Mourinho arrived at Inter in 2008 with the task of ending the club's long wait for European glory. In just two seasons, Mourinho delivered on that promise, leading Inter to an unprecedented treble in 2010, which included the Serie A title, the Coppa Italia, and the UEFA Champions League. Mourinho's Inter was a well-drilled, tactically astute team that could adapt to any opponent. His ability to motivate players and his tactical acumen were on full display during the 2010 Champions League campaign, particularly in the semi-final victory over Barcelona. Mourinho's legacy at Inter is that of a manager who brought out the best in his players and led the club to its greatest triumph.

Roberto Mancini (2004-2008, 2014-2016)

Roberto Mancini played a pivotal role in revitalizing Inter Milan in the mid-2000s. Taking over in 2004, Mancini led Inter to three consecutive Serie A titles from 2006 to 2008, as well as two Coppa Italia victories. His ability to build a cohesive and winning team laid the groundwork for the club's future successes. Mancini's tenure was marked by the return of Inter Milan to the top of Italian football after a period of underachievement. He was also instrumental in developing young talents and bringing a modern, attacking style of play to the club. Mancini's influence extended beyond his first stint, as he returned to the club in 2014, helping to stabilize the team during a challenging period.

Antonio Conte (2019-2021)

Antonio Conte's impact on Inter Milan was immediate and transformative. Appointed in 2019, Conte took over a team that had been underperforming and turned them into a powerhouse. His meticulous attention to detail, tactical discipline, and high-intensity style of play resonated with the players and brought out the best in them. Conte's 3-5-2 formation, with a focus on defensive solidity and quick transitions, suited the squad perfectly. Under his leadership, Inter ended Juventus' nine-year dominance of Serie A by winning the 2020-2021 Scudetto, securing the club's first league title in 11 years.Antonio Conte's impact on Inter Milan was immediate and transformative. Appointed in 2019, Conte took over a team that had been underperforming and turned them into a powerhouse. His meticulous attention to detail, tactical discipline, and high-intensity style of play resonated with the players and brought out the best in them. Conte's 3-5-2 formation, with a focus on defensive solidity and quick transitions, suited the squad perfectly. Under his leadership, Inter ended Juventus' nine-year dominance of Serie A by winning the 2020-2021 Scudetto, securing the club's first league title in 11 years. Conte's success at Inter Milan not only restored the club to the top of Italian football but also further solidified his reputation as one of the most effective and demanding managers in the modern game.

These players and managers represent the heart and soul of Inter Milan. Their contributions have shaped the club's history and defined its legacy, making Inter one of the most storied and successful football clubs in the world.

Conclusion: The Future of Inter Milan—Where Do We Go from Here?

As Inter Milan looks ahead to the future, the club stands at a critical juncture, poised to build on its recent successes while navigating the challenges of modern football. The 2020s have already seen Inter return to the summit of Italian football with the 2021 Scudetto, and the club has made significant strides in reestablishing itself as a European powerhouse. However, the journey is far from over, and the future holds both opportunities and obstacles.

Predictions and Expectations for the Club's Future

The future of Inter Milan will likely be shaped by several key factors, including financial stability, player development, and continued success on the pitch. The club's acquisition by Suning Holdings and the leadership of Steven Zhang have provided a strong financial foundation, but the realities of the modern game mean that maintaining this stability will require careful management. Inter will need to balance the books while remaining competitive in both Serie A and Europe. This could involve a mix of strategic player sales, smart investments in emerging talent, and the continued development of players from the club's youth academy.

On the pitch, the expectations are high. Inter Milan will aim to defend their domestic titles and reassert their dominance in Italy, particularly as rivals like Juventus and AC Milan continue to strengthen. The club's ambitions, however, extend beyond Serie A. The ultimate goal remains European glory—adding a fourth UEFA Champions League title to their storied history. Achieving this will require not only tactical brilliance and squad depth but also the mental fortitude to compete against the best clubs in Europe.

The appointment of managers who can deliver on these expectations will be crucial. The successes under Antonio Conte and Simone Inzaghi have shown the importance of having a clear tactical vision and strong leadership. Future managerial appointments will need to align with the club's long-term strategy and ambition to ensure sustained success.

Reflection on the Club's History and Its Place in World Football

Inter Milan's history is a rich tapestry woven from countless moments of triumph, resilience, and innovation. From the glory days of the *Grande Inter* under Helenio Herrera to the modern era of global expansion and success, Inter has consistently been at the forefront of Italian and European football. The club's legacy is built on a foundation of tactical innovation, cultural significance, and a commitment to excellence that has inspired generations of fans and players alike.

Inter Milan's place in world football is secure, not just as one of Italy's most successful clubs but as a global brand with a passionate following. The club's ability to attract top talent, its iconic home at the San Siro, and its storied rivalries have made Inter a symbol of footballing tradition and innovation. As football continues to evolve, Inter Milan will undoubtedly play a key role in shaping the future of the sport, both in Italy and around the world.

In conclusion, the future of Inter Milan is bright, filled with both challenges and opportunities. The club's leadership, supporters, and players all share a common goal: to continue building on the legacy of those who came before them and to write new chapters in the history of this great club. As Inter Milan moves forward, its rich history will serve as both a guide and an inspiration, reminding everyone involved of the values that have made the club one of the most respected and successful in the world. The road ahead may be uncertain, but with the right vision, determination, and passion, Inter Milan is poised to continue its journey as one of football's true giants.

Appendix A: Timeline of Major Events in Inter Milan's History

1908: Foundation of Inter Milan

- **March 9, 1908**: Inter Milan, officially known as *Football Club Internazionale Milano*, is founded by a group of Italian and Swiss dissidents from the Milan Cricket and Football Club (now AC Milan). The club was established with the intention of welcoming foreign players, a principle reflected in its name, "Internazionale."

1910: First Serie A Title

- **1910**: Just two years after its founding, Inter Milan wins its first Serie A championship, establishing itself as a significant force in Italian football.

1928: Name Change to Ambrosiana

- **1928**: Under pressure from the Fascist regime, Inter Milan is forced to merge with Unione Sportiva Milanese and change its name to *Ambrosiana*.

1939: First Coppa Italia Win

- **1939**: Inter, still under the name Ambrosiana, wins its first Coppa Italia, adding to its growing list of honors.

1945: Return to the Name Internazionale

- **1945**: After World War II and the fall of the Fascist regime, the club reverts to its original name, *Internazionale*.

1963-1966: The Grande Inter Era

- **1963-1966**: Under manager Helenio Herrera, Inter Milan dominates European and world football. The team, known as *Grande Inter*, wins two consecutive European Cups (1964, 1965) and three Serie A titles, along with two Intercontinental Cups.

1989: Record-Breaking Scudetto

- **1989**: Inter Milan, managed by Giovanni Trapattoni, wins the Serie A title with a record 58 points in a 34-match season, a remarkable achievement during a highly competitive era.

1991, 1994, 1998: UEFA Cup Triumphs

- **1991, 1994, 1998**: Inter Milan wins the UEFA Cup (now the Europa League) three times during the 1990s, cementing its status as a powerhouse in European football.

1997: Signing of Ronaldo

- **1997**: Inter Milan breaks the world transfer record to sign Brazilian superstar Ronaldo from Barcelona. Ronaldo quickly becomes a fan favorite and one of the most iconic players in the club's history.

2006: Calciopoli Scandal and 14th Scudetto

- **2006**: Following the Calciopoli scandal, Inter Milan is awarded the 2005-2006 Serie A title. The scandal leads to a period of dominance for Inter as their main rivals, Juventus and AC Milan, face significant penalties.

2006-2010: Domestic Dominance

- **2006-2010**: Inter Milan, under the management of Roberto Mancini and later José Mourinho, wins five consecutive Serie A titles, cementing their dominance in Italian football.

2010: Historic Treble

- **2010**: Under José Mourinho, Inter Milan achieves an unprecedented treble, winning the Serie A title, the Coppa Italia, and the UEFA Champions League. The Champions League victory is particularly historic, marking Inter's first European title since 1965.

2016: Acquisition by Suning Holdings

- **2016**: Chinese conglomerate Suning Holdings acquires a majority stake in Inter Milan, bringing new financial resources and a vision for global expansion.

2021: 19th Scudetto

- **2021**: Under the management of Antonio Conte, Inter Milan wins its 19th Serie A title, ending Juventus' nine-year reign as champions. This victory marks a significant return to the top of Italian football.

2023: UEFA Champions League Final Appearance

- **2023**: Inter Milan reaches the UEFA Champions League final for the first time since 2010 but falls short against Manchester City. Despite the loss, the achievement marks Inter's resurgence on the European stage.

2024: 20th Scudetto and the Second Star

- **2024**: Inter Milan wins its 20th Serie A title, earning the right to add a second star above their crest, symbolizing two decades of league dominance.

Appendix B: Complete Honors List—Titles and Awards

Inter Milan, one of the most successful football clubs in Italy and Europe, has amassed a comprehensive collection of titles and awards throughout its illustrious history. Below is a detailed list of the major honors won by the club.

Domestic Honors

Serie A (Italian Championship)

- **Winners (20):** 1909-1910, 1919-1920, 1929-1930, 1937-1938, 1939-1940, 1952-1953, 1953-1954, 1962-1963, 1964-1965, 1965-1966, 1970-1971, 1979-1980, 1988-1989, 2005-2006, 2006-2007, 2007-2008, 2008-2009, 2009-2010, 2020-2021, 2023-2024

Coppa Italia (Italian Cup)

- **Winners (9):** 1938-1939, 1977-1978, 1981-1982, 2004-2005, 2005-2006, 2009-2010, 2010-2011, 2021-2022, 2022-2023

Supercoppa Italiana (Italian Super Cup)

- **Winners (7):** 1989, 2005, 2006, 2008, 2010, 2021, 2022

European Honors

UEFA Champions League (formerly European Cup)

- **Winners (3):** 1963-1964, 1964-1965, 2009-2010

UEFA Europa League (formerly UEFA Cup)

- **Winners (3):** 1990-1991, 1993-1994, 1997-1998

UEFA Super Cup

- **Winners (1):** 2010

International Honors

Intercontinental Cup

- **Winners (2):** 1964, 1965

FIFA Club World Cup

- **Winners (1):** 2010

Youth and Other Domestic Titles

Campionato Primavera (Italian Youth Championship)

- **Winners (10):** 1963-1964, 1965-1966, 1968-1969, 1988-1989, 2001-2002, 2006-2007, 2011-2012, 2016-2017, 2017-2018, 2021-2022

Coppa Italia Primavera

- **Winners (7):** 1976-1977, 1977-1978, 2005-2006, 2015-2016, 2017-2018, 2021-2022, 2022-2023

Supercoppa Primavera

- **Winners (2):** 2007, 2018

Torneo di Viareggio (Youth World Cup)

- **Winners (8):** 1962, 1971, 1986, 2002, 2008, 2011, 2015, 2018

Other Honors

Mitropa Cup

- **Winners (1):** 1930

Coppa delle Alpi

- **Winners (1):** 1967

Bologna Trophy

- **Winners (1):** 1953

Anglo-Italian Cup

- **Winners (1):** 1970

Bibliography and Reference List

Books

1. **Foot, John.** *Calcio: A History of Italian Football.* HarperCollins, 2007.

   - A comprehensive history of Italian football, covering the rise of Serie A and the development of major clubs, including Inter Milan.

2. **Burns, Jimmy.** *La Roja: A Journey Through Spanish Football.* Simon & Schuster, 2012.

   - While focused on Spanish football, this book provides insight into the influence of players and managers who have moved between Spain and Italy, impacting clubs like Inter Milan.

3. **Goldblatt, David.** *The Ball is Round: A Global History of Football.* Penguin Books, 2006.

   - An in-depth global history of football that touches upon the development of Italian clubs, including Inter Milan, in the broader context of world football.

4. **Wilson, Jonathan.** *Inverting the Pyramid: The History of Football Tactics.* Orion, 2008.

- A detailed exploration of football tactics, with significant coverage of the tactical innovations at Inter Milan under managers like Helenio Herrera.

5. **Mourinho, José.** *The Special One: The Dark Side of José Mourinho.* HarperSport, 2015.

    - Provides insights into Mourinho's time at Inter Milan, including his approach to management and the club's historic treble in 2010.

6. **Zanetti, Javier.** *Captain and Gentleman.* Mondadori, 2014.

    - The autobiography of Javier Zanetti, detailing his career at Inter Milan and his role in the club's successes.

7. **Mazzola, Sandro.** *Piedi a banana: La storia di un campione.* Mondadori, 2004.

    - The autobiography of Sandro Mazzola, offering a personal perspective on the *Grande Inter* era.

8. **Bozzani, Gianfranco.** *Inter 1908-2021: 113 anni di storia nerazzurra.* Inter Books, 2021.

    - A chronological history of Inter Milan, covering the club's major achievements and milestones over more than a century.

Academic Journals and Articles

1. **Dunning, Eric, and Dominic Malcolm.** "Sports Violence in Italy: Ultras, Calcio, and the Politics of Football." *Journal of Sports History*, vol. 25, no. 3, 2008, pp. 331-355.

    - An analysis of the culture of football in Italy, with a focus on the political and social dynamics that have influenced clubs like Inter Milan.

2. **Porro, Nicola, and Antonio Testa.** "The Changing Landscape of Italian Football: The Impact of Globalization and Commercialization." *European Journal of Sport Science*, vol. 9, no. 5, 2009, pp. 387-400.

    - Discusses the effects of globalization on Italian football clubs, including the impact on Inter Milan's ownership and commercial strategies.

3. **Martin, Simon.** "The Political Game: Sport and Democracy in Post-War Italy." *Contemporary European History*, vol. 11, no. 3, 2002, pp. 381-402.

- Explores the relationship between football clubs like Inter Milan and political developments in Italy during the post-war period.

Websites and Online Sources

1. **UEFA.com**. "In the Zone: Inter 1-0 Milan Performance Analysis | UEFA Champions League 2022/23." *UEFA*, 2023.

    - Detailed analysis of Inter Milan's recent performances in the UEFA Champions League, highlighting tactical approaches and key players.

2. **Football Italia**. "Inter Milan's Historic Treble Season of 2009-2010." *Football Italia*, 2010.

    - Coverage of Inter Milan's treble-winning season, with insights into key matches and player performances.

3. **Inter.it**. "The History of Inter Milan." *Official Website of FC Internazionale Milano*, 2023.

    - Official timeline and history of Inter Milan, including details on major victories, player profiles, and club milestones.

4. **ESPN**. "Inter Milan: Club Profile." *ESPN FC*, 2023.
    - Club profile with statistics, historical records, and news updates on Inter Milan.

5. **Gazzetta dello Sport**. "La Storia di Inter: Un Secolo di Vittorie e Passioni." *Gazzetta dello Sport*, 2022.
    - Comprehensive coverage of Inter Milan's history, including interviews with former players and managers.

6. **The Guardian**. "Inter Milan's Tactical Evolution: From Catenaccio to Modern Mastery." *The Guardian*, 2021.
    - Analysis of Inter Milan's tactical developments over the decades, focusing on key periods in the club's history.

Historical Archives

1. **Italian Football Federation (FIGC) Archives**.
    - Historical records and documents related to Serie A and the Coppa Italia,

including Inter Milan's participation and victories.

2. **San Siro Stadium Archives.**
   - Architectural plans, historical photographs, and event records from the San Siro stadium, documenting its role as Inter Milan's home ground.

3. **Rai Sport Archives.**
   - Footage and commentary from historical matches, including Inter Milan's European and domestic triumphs.